The Spirit

Christopher Childs

The Spirit's Terrain

Creativity,
Activism,
and Transformation

Foreword by His Holiness the Dalai Lama

Beacon Press: Boston

Beacon Press
25 Beacon Street
Boston, Massachusetts 02108–2892
http://www.beacon.org

Beacon Press books
are published under the auspices of the
Unitarian Universalist Association of Congregations

03 02 01 00 99 98   8 7 6 5 4 3 2 1

From THE POETRY OF ROBERT FROST, edited by
Edward Connery Lathem, Copyright 1945 by Robert Frost,
© 1973 by Lesley Frost Ballantine, © 1969 by Henry Holt & Co., Inc.
Reprinted by permission of Henry Holt & Co., Inc.

Text design by Wesley B. Tanner/Passim Editions
Composition by Wilsted & Taylor Publishing Services

Library of Congress Cataloging-in-Publication Data
Childs, Christopher.
    The spirit's terrain : creativity, activism, and transformation /
Christopher Childs ; foreword by His Holiness the Dalai Lama.
        p.   cm.
    Includes bibliographical references.
    ISBN: 978-0-8070-2007-4
    1. Environmentalism. 2. Environmental sciences—Philosophy.
I. Title.
GE195.C55   1998
363.7'05—dc21   97-23335

Contents

*In memory of my parents,
who, into their eighth decade,
investigated with a youngest son
such radical ideas as these.*

Foreword

by His Holiness the Dalai Lama

Christopher Childs originally called this book "Working Toward the World Garden." The phrase struck me as especially apt and useful because it implies that our relationship with the earth — and our social relationships — are full of transformative possibility. Many people feel overwhelmed by the global scale of our environmental problems. They feel concern but do not know how they can individually contribute to saving the earth. On the other hand, there is nothing daunting about taking care of a garden. What's more, a garden is a place we think of with pleasure, a place to rest and enjoy. I believe that if we change our attitudes toward the natural environment as a whole, regarding it and taking care of it as the world garden, it will be a source of joy for generations to come. A similar shift in perspective toward our social and political relations might have the same result.

In old Tibet we had laws to safeguard the hills and valleys and protect otherwise defenseless wild animals. It was a noble tradition, one that I would encourage still. Today people hunt wild animals unthinkingly, and catch fish and other sea creatures for material and monetary gain rather than for sustenance. However, if we think of our future, and of our children's future, it becomes plain that our current levels of consumption are destructive. Similarly, it is inappropriate to clutter and pollute the land

and sea with things we have discarded and no longer require. We want our legacy to be a pure and unspoilt environment.

I am confident that this book will inspire readers with the possibility of personal and social transformation. It is my hope and prayer that by understanding the interdependence of all living things, people will adapt their behavior in ways that will allow our world to flourish as a garden once more, in order that all sentient beings may happily live out their lives.

Preface

Twenty years ago, when I concluded a brief career as a teacher to embark on a performing career (as I then thought), the universe took me ever so gently by the arm and steered me onto a distinct and Graceful course without my noticing it, one that led me through the world of theatre and then out of it. The wearing of masks and the borrowing of voices can be a seductive occupation, so it took fully a decade before I began to recognize that I had a voice of my own, and that I had neglected it — that I had dreams beyond and more powerful than wrapping myself in the psychic garments of fictional characters.

The transition began with my innocently volunteering for an outdoor club's "task force" on an environmental issue — the acid precipitation affecting lakes and forests and mountains that were dear to me, places I had frequented since my New England youth. Later, under the rigorous influence of a series of seminars and workshops on commitment and creativity, I awoke to the idea that until then I had been in a sort of incubation period — engaged, to use theatrical imagery, in a kind of dress rehearsal — and that it was time to undertake more substantial work. The first way I found to apply myself was by teaching to others those things I had been taught about creativity. The second was to involve myself in the environmental movement on a full-time basis. The organization to which I was guided was Greenpeace, and that is where I remained for a long time as an activist and spokesperson.

What I brought to my activist career from my years in theatre and my education in the creative process was a profound desire to translate the laws that govern art — laws I now found to be identical to the "higher laws" extolled by Thoreau, and many others — into practical action on behalf of a better world. In one sense, periods of highly publicized internal chaos notwithstanding, Greenpeace is pretty good at that. I was surrounded there by colleagues intently focused on the planning and execution of those dramatic actions for which Greenpeace is best known, and most were actions of which Thoreau would approve. However, our conscious attention rested only occasionally on higher law. Our press releases on environmental matters referred a great deal more often to science than to *con*science, and to political realities rather than those associated with the human spirit.

My relationships with activist colleagues were generally positive, intense, and, with some notable exceptions, professional rather than personal. At the same time, and largely as an outgrowth of my researches into the human gift for creativity, I found I had a good number of personal friends outside the world of activism who were genuinely interested in the deeper aspects of human consciousness. These individuals (some avowed New Agers, some not) spent a great deal of time reflecting on, studying, and attempting to embody higher values. Yet it was (and remains) a rare and striking occasion for any of them to show up at a Greenpeace protest, or its equivalent, to bring their individual spirits to bear on some material issue affecting the earth.

This dichotomy, between activists who often shy away from assessing their work in terms of spiritual values and people keenly aware of the spirit who avoid taking certain key actions in the material world, is a source of some bemusement to me. I wonder if we can ever create a world of peace or justice or ecological health without deliberately reuniting the highest aspects of our consciousness with the more mundane — without making the material spiritual — both within ourselves as individuals and collectively.

Therefore, as I have traveled through the paired landscapes of activism and the creative process, I have been on the lookout for those rare individuals in whose lives the two are conjoined. I have also had an eye out for those who offer others effective instruction in how to establish the conjunction. I have found a number of people in both categories whom I regard as colleagues in the deepest sense. Their concepts of spirituality may or may not be expressed in conventional terms; their activism may or may not always look like that of Greenpeace or other well-known groups. Some of the instruction they offer is within old traditions, and some is at least as heretical as the teachings of Socrates ever were. Many of them appear to be intent on restating very powerful old truths in very powerful modern ways — which removes the insulation from the truth, and often renews its power to disturb. They are always, however, focused on bringing forward the very best and highest in themselves and in others, to improve the lot of everyone.

This book has its foundation in what I have learned from or been inspired to imagine by such people. It is an attempt to explore a framework of concepts which might promote the development of new forms of activism — or reinvigorate some of the older ones. It is an extension of a personal investigation into ways to bring body and soul together on both an individual and a global, collective level. And it is designed to suggest to its readers that we are *all* meant to be activists in some sphere. While my background lies primarily in environmental issues, the principles I have chosen to set out apply equally to any field; while I have touched on specific issues, ranging from the pollution of the Great Lakes basin to justice for Native Americans to the Chinese occupation of Tibet, this book is not primarily about issues, but about orientation. Its investigation of such concepts as the power of visualization and the still deeper power of vision, the real meaning of intuition, and the freedom gained by acknowledging that life need not always proceed in visibly straight lines, is meant to promote an attitude of the soul more than a formula for the mind.

The book's theme is the nearly unspeakable yearning within all of us to *create*, and the implications of fully yielding — or not — to that essential hunger in our souls. And the book's first and last message to individual readers is that the most radical, powerful act ever undertaken by any human being remains the act of committing oneself, beyond reservation, to a worthy personal mission. That is the greatest art, and the only way I know to take up residence in that Garden which is the true terrain of the spirit.

Christopher Childs may be contacted through New Eden Foundation at worldgarden@igc.org.

Paradise is where we live. . . .
This is why we tend our gardens
with such artistry.

a Buddhist monk

Chapter One

Working toward the World Garden

A gifted artist and friend once recounted the following dream:

> There was a war going on, and I was in the middle of it. I was very frightened. I was being pressed to take a side and become a part of the struggle. But I didn't want to do that. And somehow, within the dream, I was suddenly aware that I had another option. I explained that I was an artist — and I found I was then lifted up, beyond the conflict, and freed to go on with my life!
>
> It was as if I was given a sort of pass — as if artists are given an alternative to becoming involved in the fighting.

I have thought about this dream from time to time in the years since my friend told me about it. I think the dream is about the right of the creative soul to live and move above and beyond the clash of opposites which has been, for eons, the most apparent dynamic in human affairs.

I believe this dream has something to offer all of us.

It should by now be deeply evident to the human species — certainly since the space program gave us photographs of Earth as seen from space — that our home planet is, quite literally, a work of art. It should also be evident that we have a unique opportunity to be the artists who shape its future. In fact, however, the primary human orientation toward the earth remains that of the user and consumer, not the artist, and is based on the tacit assumption that planetary creation (whether it took place in seven days or not) is long since complete. In practice, with rare exceptions, we are and think of ourselves as *takers* — at best as the beneficiaries of a thoughtful Providence which has provided us with a large (if limited) quantity of resources to be exploited.

Even those who might be expected to see themselves as creators of the future — the true activists, those people who commit themselves to worthwhile causes — still primarily regard themselves not as creators, but as stewards, as caretakers, or as repairpersons. The majority of my colleagues in the environmental movement, for example, remain preoccupied either with plugging their fingers into leaking seawalls or with heading off various corporate (and political) coyotes at imaginary passes.

You can do a lot of good work from that orientation, but you can also burn yourself out very quickly. You will almost certainly experience life as a struggle between opposing sides — just as my friend dreamt of two factions, each trying to draw her into the conflict — and probably the element of joy that is the province of the creative artist will be missing from your experience. Those people whose activism lasts throughout their lifetimes, and who are most revered by those who come after them, have been and are those who know themselves to be artists. This knowledge may be conscious or it may be intuitive, but the visionary quality of their lives is clear evidence that they identify themselves as more than caretakers. They are creators. And they take joy in it.

If we are to shape a successful future for ourselves, for civilization, and for the earth, we will certainly not do it by waiting for crises to materialize and dealing with them after the fact. We will not even be able to do it by anticipating crises and finding clever ways to forestall them. No amount of cleverness in coping with our own mistakes, or preventing mistakes that are about to be made, will alone suffice to guarantee the future. Nor will any amount of heroic battling against the evil Goliaths that seem to surround us. We will have to take up a much greater challenge. We will have to set aside conflict in favor of creation.

We will have to create something entirely new here, based on a commitment to a vision which is embedded deeply in the consciousness of every human being, one so powerful that it frightens us to acknowledge its existence. It is a vision that Western society (like some others) has chosen to place safely in the distant and mythical history of Earth rather than in the future where it belongs and where we would all have to work to make it real. It is the vision of Eden.

One of the more interesting aspects of the Eden myth is the relationship it suggests between creation (in this case, Creation) and husbandry. Husbandry, in its original sense, was not management or stewardship — it was cultivation. It was growing from seed; it was nurturing; it was gardening. It was an extension of the creative act, not merely the conservation of what had already been created. And anyone who has ever planned, planted, or tended a garden can testify that the boundary line between the occupations of "artist" and "gardener" is so thin as to be non-existent. Adam and Eve before the Fall were not just caretakers on behalf of the Creator; their naming of the creatures was an extension of the ongoing process of Creation. The question of the moment is whether we have the depth of commitment required to reclaim that status.

There is little doubt that in their heart of hearts most people would *like* to take up the mission of creating an Eden on this planet. The longevity of the Eden myth (and the existence of related mythology across many cultures) testifies to its power and attraction. In the decade I spent with the crusading organization Greenpeace, I met with a good many people who disagreed (some of them quite vigorously) with our style, with our opinions on specific issues, or with our choice of tactics. But I never met with a single person who showed the slightest inclination to gainsay the vision for the world that is written into the group's name.

Everybody likes the image of Eden, but very few people work to make it manifest.

The array of excuses offered to explain why people don't roll up their sleeves and get to work — generally starting with one form or another of "We can't afford to" — is startling and impressive. So is the array of half-truths brought forth by those who claim to be building the future when they are not. The situation reminds me of Robert Penn Warren's description of the inhabitants of a sleepy Southern town in *All the King's Men*:

> You know they . . . wanted to do good things, because they
> always gave good reasons for the things they did.

People generally claim a commitment to the future which is almost universally belied by their actions. Corporations (a particular focus of the wrath of most environmentalists) engage broadly and often hideously in the act of "greenwashing" themselves, asserting a largely nonexistent dedication to the welfare of people and of the environment; governments protest that they are "doing their best" (whatever that means to them) to protect the long-term welfare of the land and the citizenry; individuals maintain that they are giving as much time (and money) to worthy causes as they can possibly afford. Unsurprisingly, nobody strides darkly forward to say that he or she opposes preserving the environment, advancing the welfare of the world's poor, or creating a just and peaceable world society; yet it is a fact that most people are contributing daily, in ways small or large, to the likely degradation of the planet's future. They subscribe to the image of Eden but deny — actually or effectively — the possibility of bringing the reality into being.

Until the accepted model for the human relationship to the earth is changed from stewardship to creativity, that situation is likely to persist.

Chapter Two

The Problem of
Activism as Theatre

Before I became seriously involved in environmental and peace activism, I was for fifteen years involved in the theatre. I designed sets, directed once or twice, chaired an advisory panel to a state arts council, sat on the board of a short-lived theatre for new plays, and, above all, acted. I had the good fortune to play classical roles, and to take part in plays, independent film productions, and two Public Television miniseries based in American history. I also wrote and performed a one-man "stage portrait" of Henry David Thoreau.

Today I rarely set foot onstage, having found myself preoccupied with what seem to me to be more direct means of improving the world. But occasionally my commitment to activism does intersect what remains of my investment in acting. Not long ago, I revived my Thoreauvian portrait for a pair of outdoor performances in a spectacular grotto high above the Pacific, as a fundraiser for a coalition that is attempting to save Los Angeles's last remaining fragment of coastal wetlands from development. A hundred or two souls ("with their bodies," as Thoreau would have said) made the winding trek up from the Pacific Coast Highway into the mountains overlooking the Malibu coastline, took in the stunning view of the ocean far below, and the sunset, and afforded the piece a supportive audience. The mini-amphitheatre where I played (survivor of two major fires in three years) was made available to us gratis by its owners, the architect Eric Lloyd Wright (grandson of Frank) and his artist wife, Mary.

The patent irony in these goings-on was that the proposed development amid the wetlands, Playa Vista, included the DreamWorks studio of Steven Spielberg and company, who had also become full partners in building the "mini-city" (their term) that would accompany the studio. So I was in the position of both 1) offering a theatrical event that contravened some material aspirations of one of the world's leading masters of theatricality, and 2) embodying my own concept of creative activism in direct opposition to one of the planet's most publicly acknowledged creators. All this was taking place in a location offered by an artist and by an architect who was a descendant of another of the culture's most legendary creative spirits. The whole thing raised large and deeply interesting questions both about the responsibility of creators and, for me, about the function of drama in a healthy society. It deepened through direct experience my understanding of a comment made fifty years ago by playwright Arthur Miller: "I could not imagine a theatre worth my time that did not want to change the world." And it reminded me that my theatrical involvement with Thoreau had subtly ushered me into activism in the first place.[1]

Western theatre began in close association with religion and was, to an extent, its handmaiden for early Greek audiences. But in contemporary culture the profession has been degraded to such an extent that few actors can, over the course of a career, point with genuine pride to even one role in ten as reflecting or embodying great ideals or true spiritual values. (I do not choose that figure quite arbitrarily; I am translocating a statistic offered by Richard Burton when he said that a contemporary actor was fortunate if he could count perhaps ten percent of his work as artistically successful.) The performance in the Malibu hills underscored for me that this diminution of the quality of theatre, and of its beneficial influence on the spirit, carries a message about the dynamic from which our values now arise. It also holds a lesson for activists.

At the core of this process of degradation, I think, is a shift in the focus of audiences and artists from the drama as a *vehicle for ideals* to the drama as a means of stimulating emotional response. But how can we ever progress toward an ideal world unless we acknowledge and confront our ideals? We revere the great, old plays because while they tell great stories, they never let us forget that there is something at stake that is actually larger than the physical life and physical death of their characters. Go see Kenneth Branagh's grand movie version of *Hamlet* and you will surely be reminded that the play is not a murder mystery, nor for that matter is it a play about the psychological evolution of a particularly intelligent and interesting young man under great stress. It is a play about destiny, about the accurate recognition and interpretation of messages originating with God, and about coming to terms with one's own material mortality while accepting that other dimensions of reality do, in fact, exist which are of greater weight and moment than the apparent ones. The murder mystery or (for the more cerebral) the psychological investigation may be the hooks that get some of us to the theatre. But it is the investigation of the Doings of the Divine that keeps us talking and thinking about the play after we leave.[2]

Deepak Chopra has characterized contemporary society as "hysterical and melodramatic." The words are strong, but Chopra makes the characterization seem matter-of-fact, which indeed it is. The world in which today's drama exists in all its manifestations — and with which it shares a sort of continuous feedback loop — is one that routinely favors and rewards some form of melodrama over more substantive events or the reporting of events. This shows up vividly in the pathetic devolution of television news programs, over the last forty years or so, from real journalism (as embodied in the work of Edward R. Murrow, for example) to shoddy tabloid diversion. Ironically and not coincidentally, a onetime actor of my acquaintance now hosts one of the most popular tabloid news programs. My affection for an old colleague notwithstanding, this symbolic wedding of the actor's talents and experience with a dominant contemporary journalistic form should give us pause. Contrast for yourself *Hard Copy* with *Hamlet*.

The sorry truth of the matter is that almost across the spectrum our culture has elected to value sensation over the deep and genuine theatricality that lies at the heart of important events and movements. People respond to the emotional cattle prod — which should make it a matter of little surprise when television and film writers, directors, and producers treat audiences pretty much like cattle. (They often enough treat actors that way, too.)[3] This situation is no more healthy or joyful for those wielding the prod than it is for the rest of us. Another onetime colleague of mine, with multiple talents as writer, actor, and producer, recently made a career of turning (melo)dramatic public events into television movies; at last report, he had grown so weary of this enterprise that he laid down the law and said he wouldn't write another sensationalized treatment for any of the networks — they could take his own fictional work or nothing at all.

All of this destructive tendency to weigh superficial melodrama over something more profound is based in a central misperception, one which is shared by a great many serious playwrights as well as tabloid journalists: the belief that drama subsists fundamentally in the conflict of opposing forces. As a corollary, they believe that the dramatic "catharsis" first specified by Aristotle is a phenomenon merely of the emotions, proceeding from the buildup of emotional tension in the audience and its sympathetic release as the conflict-driven plot resolves itself. But the process of plot-bound emotional release goes no nearer to the heart of drama than the crackling of a short-wave radio receiver goes to the core of the mystery of light.

The majority of us have allowed ourselves to become addicts to the cheap thrill of spectatorship at the conflicts in human existence, instead of players in the real game of shaping life. We become voyeurs instead of creators. It is not just a matter for concern in theatre and movies, or television news programming — we are conflict junkies in our everyday, "real" lives as well. In this scheme of things, any experience that excites the psyche and generates some inner sensation of conflict gains a measure of respectability. We consciously reject the horrific while unconsciously giving it a place, literally, of great regard — that is, by *regarding* at length that which intensely stimulates our emotions, we give it weight to influence our consciousness in unknown and unobserved ways. We *think* we are valuing that which is good and constructive and harmonious with the needs of spirit, and rejecting and discarding that which is ugly and destructive; we *are* in fact sending ourselves a message, conscious or not, that conflict is entertainment.

Our cultural misperception about the nature of drama extends its careless tentacles well into the world of social activism. The idea that conflict is entertainment ultimately encompasses not only conflicts between or among people, but inner conflicts of values or concepts, the clash of apparently irreconcilable points of view, and the interaction between humans and nature.[4] People responded intensely (pro or con) to the doomsday imagery of the antinuclear movement precisely because it had the conflict-inducing power of a cattle prod. Over time, people become not only jaded in their response to such imagery, but justifiably angry with those of us who abuse it. Nobody is happy when they are sucked into a process that demeans them, even if they do not clearly or consciously recognize what is going on beneath the surface of the relationship. There is a clear distinction between setting forth a clinical description of the negative consequences of certain unwise actions — accompanied by a positive alternative — on the one hand, and using such a description as a manipulative device, on the other.

When activists publicize negative trends, *intention is everything*. And it's no good lying about it, especially to oneself. Someone who is honestly dedicated to awakening the public to an important truth, and especially to stimulating the public's creative spirit over the long term, will learn to minimize the tendency to melodrama and overstatement. He or she will come to understand that you take advantage of an addict at your own risk. The true visionary sets forth the vision and the facts, and allows them to speak for themselves without mindless embellishment. The arts to be called into play are poetry and journalism, not melodrama.

Please understand that when I speak of an addiction to the outwardly dramatic in society and refer to the majority of people as "conflict junkies," I am speaking literally. The human psychological and physiological mechanism is such that we can become attached, very much without realizing it, to certain sets of stimuli (inducing pleasure or pain) and the effects they produce in us, at the expense of an awareness of those deeper stimuli and effects that ultimately give life meaning. The mechanism by which such psychotropic substances as heroin gain a foothold in human consciousness is in fact a replica of, or substitute for, a mechanism by which we normally experience pleasure. Again, such processes are not the deepest or most fundamental in human consciousness — contrary to a common assumption — yet in the absence of a deeper understanding of the principles by which consciousness actually works, these shallower mechanisms generally hold sway.

The mechanism by which we experience warning or alarm is an interesting variant on the mechanisms of pleasure and pain. It carries with it some of the implications of the pain mechanism, but because it precedes events, it contains also the seeds of pleasure, which may appear in the form of feelings of relief when injury is successfully avoided or disaster forestalled. This has its own addictive potential. Producers of horror movies are well acquainted with the public's desire to experience feelings of sheer terror — as long as the terror is ultimately resolved or, to use the classic theatrical term, "purged." A significant point here is that once the human "alarm system" is brought into play, it gives rise to the base expectation that *some* resolution will occur, and that whatever the danger at hand, the individual can probably do something about it (or, in the case of horror movies, the producer will arrange for something to be done on the audience's behalf).

For precisely this reason, the mechanism of alarm is an unreliable resource for deliberate, long-term, repeated manipulation by an outside agency. When an alarm is raised and the experience of resolution does not follow pretty quickly, the human animal may come to distrust or even discard the particular form of alarm in question. This is especially true when the person being alarmed does not feel capable of taking a constructive part in such a resolution. Most of the issues raised by activist movements are not susceptible to easy, short-term resolution, by individuals or by society. When activists take advantage of the psychological mechanism of alarm, they are thus in a strategically vulnerable position: they stimulate short-term expectations, however unconscious, which are rarely fulfilled. Any activist who wonders why apocalyptic imagery generates a backlash can find at least a crude analogy in his or her personal reaction the next time he or she is in the vicinity of an automobile theft alarm when it goes off.

This analysis may raise the hackles of many a hard-core Western activist. And I am, in truth, questioning the deeper intentions of some of the people who have worked and are working at the business of pointing out the many weaknesses and failures of society, because some of them are undermining the very work they claim to advance. But my judgment is not formulaic: there are people doing very similar things in the activist universe who in fact have at bottom very different intentions, and it can take the wisdom of Solomon to distinguish the best from the worst. In the absence of a definitive formula for assessing who is genuine in intent and who is not, it is reasonable as a first step to ask, Who is being manipulative, and who is just giving us the best available facts? If activists want to maintain a place in the public consciousness over time, they will have to establish themselves as members of the second group. For example, few things have served Greenpeace as well as its track record, especially in recent years, in the area of ferreting out information — and scientific prognostications — that ultimately prove accurate.[5] Highly public confrontations with industry and authority may put the group in the headlines, but it is its diligent research in the archives of science, government, and corporations that keeps reporters talking to Greenpeace campaigners even when the organization's name is off the front page.

And what gives confrontation meaning and power, in any case, is not the outward style of the event, but the truth the confrontation is designed to reveal. The Quaker concept of "bearing witness," which Greenpeace has specifically borrowed since its earliest days and which permeates Western activism, nowhere suggests, promotes, or implies the least focus on melodrama for its own sake — rather the opposite. Again, intention is everything. When an activist's consciousness of the drama in adversarial contact outweighs his or her dedication to genuine risk taking on behalf of the truth, that individual takes a stand on very shaky ground.

The true moral, spirited urge to confront and oppose destructive and corrosive forces is a tonic to the soul, but it is not focused on conflict for conflict's sake, and it is most certainly not aimed at entertainment. It arises from the deep desire to further the creative process. It focuses on diverting energies which threaten to disrupt that process and ultimately on redirecting them to constructive ends. Such an urge involves the willingness to take evident risks without the desire to do harm to anyone — rather the opposite, with the wish only that an adversary turn his or her efforts to good rather than to ill — and its exercise is the way of the creator who is only incidentally, if at all, a warrior. It pits the individual *against* an antagonist in the structural sense that a dam is placed against a flood. It is an urge essential to activism (which, without it, can shortly turn to well-intentioned mush), but outward *forms* of opposition or antagonism or conflict have very little intrinsically to do with this genuine urge to confront.

We are of necessity in the business, ultimately, of promoting a unified advance of the human species — not sentimentally unified, but unified at a more fundamental level. It may be true that not everyone will be prepared to join in that advance. But it is a very dicey business, along the way, to drive any more wedges between people than absolutely necessary. I never wish to stand before the doors (or the discharge pipes, for that matter) of a corporation without reminding myself that there are many people therein who might perfectly well, under other life circumstances, have wound up doing what I am doing. I do not conceive of Gandhi, or Dr. King, or Mother Teresa standing before the doors of any institution and hating the people inside, nor even wishing to deliberately dramatize their differences with those people for effect.

This is a delicate but crucial distinction. I am not discarding

the advantages offered by an eye-catching style of protest, but
there are ways and then there are ways to employ one's sense of
style. If style in fact outweighs one's deepest and highest sense
of substance at any point, this should be cause for some serious
reexamination. And if the true substance is not there, the one
course of conscience is to simply walk away.

Some years ago, after flying about the country at length, speaking to college students, I gained that exalted status with one air-
line which allows frequent fliers to take a vacant first-class seat
when booked in coach. So it was that one day I found myself en
route back to Los Angeles seated in first class next to a senior
official of the Arco Corporation. (This was at precisely the time
when Greenpeace had produced a particularly effective public
service announcement prophesying the ultimate demise of the
automobile and, by extension, the oil industry which feeds it.)
There being no accidents in life, I thought I should seize the opportunity, and I overcame my reserve sufficiently to carry on a
conversation. In the course of our talk it occurred to me to ask
about the sale of Arco's solar division, which had once been a
glimmering light in the dark landscape of an industry associated
with everything from global warming to the Gulf War.

I remember clearly this man's expression as he spoke of how
he had once been a part of that division of the company, how it
had been insufficiently profitable to satisfy the short-term demands of the company's shareholders and the corporate captains, and how much he had enjoyed working there before the division was sold. I doubt seriously that he had ever admitted,
even to himself, the depth of the sadness that I now clearly perceived in his eyes. There are adversarial points of view in life,

and it is folly to ignore them or to fail to identify an individual adversary who stands in one's path, but it is my training and my preference to view an adversary as one who in the long run may be the greatest beneficiary of my own dedication to a worthy ideal. My compatriots and I were not trying to put Arco out of business; whether or not they stay in business is up to them. We were, however, attempting to develop a momentum in society such that they could only stay in business by transforming business itself. In the end, only such a holistic transformation will restore well-being and integrity to those who work for such corporations.

Few things would please me more than to see that Arco executive back at work overseeing the production of solar arrays — or any other visionary product which it gave him joy to offer the public. I deeply wish him well and I acknowledge the lesson he presented.

When one begins to understand the "power of the picture" — the potency of visualization and the implications of planting exaggerated images of crisis in the public mind — the imagery of apocalypse starts to look like a very limited investment indeed. Its abuse suggests recourse to a rather dark side of theatre — an approach very different from the process by which great theatre sows the seeds of hope, or perhaps something even better and stronger, in the hearts of its audience.

True drama resides in the conjoined elements of beauty and truth, neither of which is intrinsically bound up with any process of conflict. Both are inherently dramatic. If you have any doubts about that, I offer with some seriousness this exercise: spend ten minutes contemplating a sunrise, and ten more reflecting on the last nine paragraphs of *Walden*. A major corollary of the needed shift in orientation in the world is that we must abandon the human addiction to the superficially dramatic in favor of a genuine appreciation of both truth and beauty, of the human ability to perceive them, and of the astounding gift of being able to bring beauty into existence. The essence of drama will be found in these places. It is time to correct our perception.

Only by moving away from a definition which associates drama with the literal or figurative bashing of heads and the resolution of emotional conflict, to a definition which correctly apprehends drama as residing in the fulfillment of the great creative urge, and the laws by which it proceeds, can we hope to unify the human species in the work of building the Garden. At its worthy best, activism returns to such an original and idealistic definition of theatricality, and draws attention to a cause strictly on the basis of its highest merit. What attracts the consciousness of the public in the short term may be style, but only if that style emerges spontaneously from an intense commitment to substance will it hold people's attention. In practice, it is one of the greatest challenges of activism to remain rigorously focused on the truth at the heart of the cause — so focused that the universe literally springs to our aid and provides processes and means that may have been nowhere visible at the time the original commitment was made.

The use of manipulative devices of any kind — technological or psychological—forecloses the option of achieving results through faith. For those of us who take activism to be a matter of the spirit first and material process second, this is not a small point.

Chapter Three

Sculpture Earth/
Symphony Earth

During my first summer of full-time employment with Greenpeace, I spent several intense weeks involved in a series of nonviolent "direct actions" that targeted major polluters in the Great Lakes. In the midst of this I met a couple in northern Ohio who opened their home to us, and I have not forgotten their kindness — nor their dedication to the idea of restoring the health of Lake Erie and its surrounding environment, where they and their children live. The husband worked as a landscaper on a small scale, planting flowers and shrubbery around the homes of others, effecting a transformation of the land piece by piece.

This family, who were not wealthy, lived next to an old and well-worn Catholic church, of which they were the caretakers. It has always been striking to me that the same people who were working to keep a church alive were the people laboring to keep nature alive in their community. It says to me something about what religion is supposed to imply when there is still spirit alive within it.

I do not mean to romanticize the existence of these people. While dealing with the gritty and immediate challenges of making a life for themselves and five children — in a town where up to one-third of the population has been unemployed in recent years — they somehow retained a sufficiently concentrated focus on long-term values to invest a significant quantity of time, effort, and psychic energy in protecting and improving the planet. Their activism, God knows, offered them no direct material gain, did little to enhance their popularity in the community (except among a handful of like-minded souls), and subjected them to certain real risks — especially when they kept company with the likes of Greenpeace activists, who tend to generate controversy.

What does it take to be the kind of person who, matter-of-factly and absent applause, embodies this type of commitment? I suspect — though I cannot prove it, and the assertion may indeed be unprovable — that more than any one other skill, this sort of dedication requires some innate ability to *picture* a desirable future. I do not necessarily mean that the ability has to be a conscious one; I think only that such individuals have a mechanism active somewhere within their consciousness to which they turn, perhaps intuitively rather than deliberately, for inspiration. And I suspect that this mechanism relies on a language of visual imagery.

The beauty and poetry of religious texts, and the practice of prayer, may have once been primary sources of this imagery. A genuine religious practice takes a person beyond the limited concerns of the ego and embeds deeply in his or her consciousness a picture of what God (in Western terms) intended the world to be like. This picture may be offset, especially in a context of fundamentalism, by apocalyptic images and a belief in an inevitable and violent passing of this world. In general, however, such embedded, positive, sacred imagery is extraordinarily resilient and has great, if latent, power.

Again, I do not think that people have necessarily to be *conscious* of the imagery — not continuously, at any rate — nor aware of the role it plays. But I believe there is a partly clinical or structural reason why great activists tend to be deeply religious, or certainly deeply spiritual. Such people carry about with them, as a constant resource in their lives, the imagery of Eden or its equivalent in their personal spiritual traditions. And that imagery, particularly in a grounded individual who remains aware of existing realities, can draw forth remarkable creative energy.

Despite the rise of fundamentalism, this is not an age in which religion is a deeply functional force in the lives of most Westerners. If my premise is correct, then, for many people a means of establishing powerful, positive, personal and global imagery in their consciousness must be sought out by choice: an enlightened religion is not sufficiently present in the lives of most people to do the job for them.

I have both studied and taught techniques of creative visualization, the practice of inwardly and deliberately "seeing" successful results from the moment one sets out to achieve them. This approach is now used consistently by such highly visible figures as Olympic divers (who can often be observed, eyes closed, visualizing a perfect dive just before striding forward on the board or platform). It is also used in the treatment of serious illness, most commonly in conjunction with conventional Western medical practice, as a stimulus to the body's immune system: people undergoing chemotherapy are often encouraged to imagine tumors becoming smaller and ultimately disappearing. There is floating about the culture by now a good deal of evidence — in the experience of everyone from athletes and cancer patients to artists, architects, and even computer software designers — that such focused imagery has tremendous power to affect the psyche, and to directly or indirectly effect results in the physical world. This bit of knowledge, however, has not been grasped by many in the activist community, nor by the average person who would like to contribute to the improvement of things.

My opinions on the subject of creative visualization are quite strong. I have been known to tell activists that if they are working *without* deliberately visualizing their goals, they are in the position of a carpenter who chooses to build a house using a stone in place of a hammer. (He may be able to complete the project, but at what wasted cost of time, temper, and professionalism?) We know that public attention is routinely held by images of war, disease, starvation, and natural and unnatural disaster. If we claim an active concern about the future, we had better plant some powerfully positive, counterbalancing imagery both in our own minds and in the consciousness of others. We have to take the time to *envision* how we want things to turn out, and to transmit that vision by every conceivable means to every available audience. The importance of planting the seeds, at least, of a workable vision in the public mind cannot be overestimated. For even beyond the conscious use of positive imagery, it is highly probable that successful people habitually visualize results even when they are unaware of the process.

There are particular images and concepts already in the public consciousness that can be successfully expanded to serve a creative activism. For example, the most durable metaphor (and perhaps the best) of the modern, stewardship-based environmental movement may be that of Buckminster Fuller's "spaceship Earth." After the Apollo moon missions showed us the planet, and ourselves, from a new, distinct, and dramatic perspective, the spaceship image served as a unique point of entry into environmental concerns, nuclear disarmament, and other social causes for thousands of people. Few phrases have so well fulfilled their linguistic mission.

But Fuller's image stops a little short, I think, of inspiring real artistry in most people. The Apollo program gave us another memorable metaphor — offered by Michael Collins, who gazed through his spacecraft window on the Apollo 11 mission and saw Earth as "a jewel against the black sky" of space — which hints at the kind of imagery that might best serve a creativity-based activism. If Earth as spaceship commands our attention to its maintenance and preservation, Earth as jewel moves us a step closer to seeing and appreciating it as a work of art.

It's not original to point out that the word "art" can be found literally at the core of the word "ea*rt*h," nor to say that we would serve the planet better, and ourselves, if we truly took the connection to heart. Part of what is needed to turn this insight into functional influence in society is to expand Michael Collins's imagery. A jewel appears complete and static, while a planet is dynamic and unfinished until the day its raw material is reclaimed by the cosmos. We need a way of relating to the earth that retains the astronaut's sense of its exquisite rarity and beauty, and simultaneously evokes an awareness that it is a work of art which is unfinished — and that we are among its potential authors, composers, or sculptors.

Certain works of art convey a predominant sense of visual beauty; others, one of dynamism. Paintings and sculpture tend, logically enough, toward the former; music, toward the latter.

Neither analogy is likely to soon displace the image of spaceship Earth in the popular imagination, but there are as many good reasons to imagine the planet as a painting or a sculpture or a symphony, as to see it as a spaceship.[1] And these models have much power. There is a reason why many a garden has been described as a "symphony of color": the metaphor conveys the complex, *active* interrelationship among the many elements and processes of the whole. The creativity-based activism I am talking about will encourage and inspire people to be far more aware of the interactions among the elements of nature *and* to value far more greatly their own contribution to the whole. The concept of the planet as symphony supports both aims.

One of the useful implications of a musical analogy is that it suggests both structure and spontaneity. We think of music as composition, created according to certain principles and laws, yet immensely flexible and responsive to the impact of individuals. (A great symphony is, of course, never actually played quite the same way twice.) If we are to relinquish the broadly accepted idea that the earth, or existing political and social relations, are a *fait accompli* — that humanity has some unique right to manipulate the existing planet but is not really able or allowed to create anew here and that we therefore can at best hope to be preservationists — we must entertain some perception equivalent to life as a symphony-in-progress *and* make a commitment to taking a worthy part in it. The former orientation makes us users, and, more often than not, abusers; the latter makes us composers, conductors, writers, true inventors and artists.

And we cannot effectively grasp this notion of the planet as a work of art without simultaneously seeing our individual lives as works of art as well. For hand in hand with the experience of the earth or human society as something long-finished goes the experience of our own lives as determined, largely or entirely, by external forces. How many people ever consciously and seriously entertain the possibility of their lives as works of beauty and lasting significance, of which they are the primary shapers, with external forces only secondary players in the game? How many who have toyed with the notion of individual creativity have missed the larger point: gaining personal creative power and skills is useless unless these are put to work in the genuine service of what is beautiful, unselfish, and true.

You can think of your life as you might think of a great painting, or a piece of music, or a garden, or any other work of real genius, and it will have largely the same effect. Let me make it clear that I am proposing this as a literal and (self-)disciplined exercise. Its point is both to enhance your sense that you *can* shape your own life and to acknowledge the degree of artistry required to improve the life of the greater, cumulative work that is the tapestry of reality on earth. The useful but overworked phrase "Think globally, act locally" turns out to apply in this context either as written or reversed: to approach your own life with genuine and committed artistry inevitably implies contributing positively to the global work; to make a real commitment to the planet as a whole will, as inevitably and beneficially, affect the shape and progress of your life as an individual soul immersed in the symphony.

If you are prepared to take this idea — and this book — seriously, please do the following exercise right now. Put the book down for a moment, close your eyes, and envision your life as a work of whatever sort of art you prefer. Envision it literally, metaphorically, evocatively, or however you wish. But come up with a series of pictures or sound images that convey the essence of what you want life to be like for you. (If it were a painting, what would it look like? If it were a dance, what form would it take? If it were a piece of music, how might it sound?) This is not a time to indulge in shyness, or debate, or perfectionism; just find something that captures a significant part of what you'd like your life to represent. Just put the book down — wherever you are — close your eyes, and imagine.

And when you're done thinking about your own life as a work of art (which may take a few seconds, a few minutes, or a few grandly indulgent hours), do the same thing for the planet on which your life depends.

Go on, do it. Put the book down *now.*

Chapter Four

Transforming the Struggle

Each February in some major city, from Nashville to Chicago to Los Angeles, hundreds of college students and program staff gather for the annual convention of the National Association for Campus Activities. Joining them is a small army of speakers, rock musicians, comedians, magicians, and other entertainers seeking engagements at American (and some Canadian) colleges and universities. It is a unique, kaleidoscopic, portable microcosm of contemporary culture.

The serious lecturers, much the minority group at these affairs, tend to create small temporary communities there. And in such fleeting villages of common interest I have met remarkable people, from veterans of the Chinese student movement and Tiananmen Square to anti-apartheid activists (before the old system crumbled) from South Africa, to powerful speakers on environmental racism in the Deep South (and the Midwest, and elsewhere) in America.

One year I had the opportunity to meet Martin Luther King III. We sat in a hotel room and talked of the relationship between issues of environmental justice and the work of transforming race relations in this country. I was grateful for the company and the conversation, in a hotel in midwinter far from home and family. I was also grateful for the opportunity to get to know the man. The quiet presence of the inevitable bodyguards (though they gently withdrew to the next room) made it impossible to forget the legacy he had inherited, with its tapestry of darkness and light interwoven; yet the simplicity of his manner set the legacy, for the moment, a little to one side.

Given the experiences of his family from his childhood on, and, most of all, given the death of his father, no one could have more cause to show bitterness toward another race or toward society in general. But I saw no bitterness in his eyes and heard not a trace of it in his voice or words. If the burden borne by his father and mother had been taken up largely by conscious choice, the younger Martin and his siblings had inherited it at birth; their graciousness of carriage is thus tribute to their native spirit as well as their parents' love and example. Martin's oratorical gift is not his father's, but it is rare enough in its own right, and I was glad that he was speaking on the college circuit. It was well worth the students' time and attention to experience his kindliness of spirit and his lack of animosity or smallness of mind or heart.

In my present line of work I have had many occasions to reflect on the brighter part of the legacy this man had inherited and had embraced. That part of the tapestry, I knew, extended back to Gandhi and Thoreau, and beyond them, as far as Jesus and Hillel, and presumably to teachers whose names are long since lost to us. All were visionaries who remained grounded in the realities of their times, retrieving again and again a focus on some great good that they understood was waiting to be brought into the world. No doubt they all grasped the intrinsic relationship between choices made within one's personal sphere and one's influence on the world at large. One reads of Gandhi's decision to eliminate sugar from his own diet after being approached by a mother who was worried about her young son's consumption of the stuff: Gandhi knew he could have a genuine influence on the boy only if he were speaking and acting from a place of complete integrity in his own life. It was a transaction of the spirit first, rendered in the material only thereafter.

Perhaps all such great historical contributors to the gracefully woven fabric of peaceful, creative change needed to be confronted with a particular problem before their inner resources could be brought to bear in the world. But I do not think they were "problem solvers" in the ordinary sense. The challenges they faced became exquisite stimuli for the full emergence of their spirits in the world, and the product of that emergence was not "planetary maintenance" — not stewardship — but transformation. For such people, the world's injustices are not finally problems to be solved, they are realities to pass through, or beyond, in the process of shaping a world significantly different from the one in which the weavers of the tapestry find themselves.

In a single, legendary speech, Martin Luther King, Jr., simultaneously reminded the world of how far it rested from the goals of equality and justice *and* evoked the vision of a fulfilled world so powerfully that millions of people instantly recognized it as not only a possibility but perhaps an inevitability. It was artistry of a very, very high order. This juxtaposition of what is and a clarified, deeply poetic vision of what can be lies at the heart of the creative process. It mobilizes the spirit at a level beyond mere good behavior. It has struck me that there is a relationship between this truth and the fact that Dr. King apparently shared with his children not just a tradition of behavior but an orientation of the spirit.

That student activities convention was one (and I have been to quite a few) that I left richer than I came. I felt I had been exposed to an inheritance of goodness and creativity that had staying power.

The necessity of remaining grounded in existing realities while insistently acknowledging the *possibility* of achieving a goal has been remarked on by both artists and theorists. The general model of the creative process suggests that by accurately representing the world of today while stubbornly holding out a genuine vision of a better future, we generate the field of creative energy that is implied in the famous quote from Goethe:

> Whatever you can do, or dream you can, begin it.
> Boldness has genius, power and magic in it.

A less poetic but more detailed and analytical model of the creative process is offered by teacher, writer, and composer Robert Fritz, author of *The Path of Least Resistance*. He characterizes the energy existing between an accurate awareness of the present and a worthwhile vision of tomorrow as *structural tension*. This energy is psychologically neutral, and not to be confused with the usual experience of tension shared by most of us when we are attempting to change things — especially, perhaps, when we are treating challenges as problems to be solved or adversaries to be overwhelmed rather than as creative stimuli, springboards to greater "practical visionary" accomplishments.

You can get an introductory sense, at least, of the nature of structural tension by doing the following exercise. Close your eyes and picture some goal or result you've been focusing on lately — preferably, for purposes of the exercise, a minor rather than a major one. When you have established a clear picture representing that goal or result, set it aside for a moment and concentrate instead on where you stand now relative to the goal. Is it something you've made progress toward? If so, what progress remains to be made? Try to summarize in a mental snapshot your honest report to yourself of how far you have (and haven't) come. Then, when the picture is reasonably clear, try to bring into your mind that previously formed picture of the goal *and hold it simultaneously* in your consciousness. You'll probably find it challenging, but to the extent you're able to hold both images in your mind at the same time, you will likely sense some part of the energy that resides between the two. If you wish to gain real mastery in this type of creative focus, I refer you to the seminars (and audiotapes) of Robert Fritz, on which this exercise is based. But this example may at least give you a taste of structured creating.

Something else Fritz makes clear is that the human tendency to wait for an externally imposed "jump-start" before making significant improvements in our lives, or in the fabric of society, is a dangerous way to do business on this planet. Though good people, once startled into action, often go on to do great things — and sometimes learn to transcend the orientation that held them in thrall to "crisis response" in the first place — our species needs to make a major, planet-wide transition from the stimulus of bad experiences to the stimulus of wise, intuitive, intelligent foresight.

The distinction between these orientations is powerfully articulated in Fritz's writing and in his many courses and workshops on creativity. The old approach, which he characterizes as the reactive-responsive orientation, needs to be supplanted by the *orientation of the creative*. He makes it clear that the former orientation manifested in the life of an individual "has such built-in structural limitations that it is impossible for you to be a master of your life-building process." The orientation of the creative, on the other hand — when an individual is truly prepared to enter into it — engages us with that domain of consciousness in which, upon respectful entry, mastery can become inevitable.

I can testify personally to the transformative potential of this approach: it was the work of Robert Fritz that propelled me into serious activism. It also clarified for me why, even in my previous volunteer environmental efforts, I had had an intuitive resistance to dramatizing negative images rather than letting the negative speak for itself within a more holistic context.

There are significant practical limitations of a reactive-responsive approach in activism. One of them is the inevitable backlash, evidenced in many conservative movements, that is generated by the tendency to lean on negative or even apocalyptic imagery to provoke public response. Another is the mental and spiritual numbness that sets in — after years of hearing how bad things have become and how much worse they may get — even among many of the sympathetic public.[1] This last is related to what one newsman, concerned at falling ratings for television newscasts filled with images of death and destruction, has called "disaster fatigue," but it goes deeper than that. Instead of making people feel more powerful by letting them know the facts, many activists have risked contributing to Thoreau's phenomenon of "quiet desperation" — or worse — and a feeling of *dis*empowerment. It is for such reasons that the old ways of doing business are not getting the results they used to, and the impli-

cations for the future of activism — and of humanity and the
planet — are large.

The problem lies in the attempt to use negative conclusions
about the possible future, however wisely or well reasoned, as a
manipulative device. Human consciousness is a resilient me-
dium, and it has a tremendous, built-in resistance to being
pushed into a configuration that does not serve the well-being of
the human spirit: even if one tries to manipulate it into a certain
shape with what seem the very best of intentions, it will not in-
definitely allow itself to remain in a shape that interferes with its
higher welfare.[2] Spiritual welfare requires the freedom to aspire
to a state of human consciousness which is Edenic in the sense
that it is *natively creative.* For that very powerful reason, even the
highest-minded efforts to force the human spirit into a reactive
or responsive mode must eventually falter.

The lesson for activism ought to be patent. People will respond less vigorously to the alarm bell over time, especially
when the alarm (as in the case of global climate change, for example) calls them to address a problem they cannot clearly discern on their own, the solution to which appears likely to involve
real sacrifices. Crises that are visible, especially if close to home,
may yet mobilize people fairly rapidly. But we are increasingly
faced with problems that are global, distant, subtle, or uncertain, at least in the public mind, in their effects. (Many are also
subject to obfuscation by those too corrupt, arrogant, or ignorant to acknowledge the importance of addressing them.) And
on a structural level, as Robert Fritz points out, *activists have
regularly used the same approach as their adversaries* in the resulting debate — jamming some manipulative lever into the
public consciousness and pushing mightily. We argue that (yet

again) swift action must be taken to prevent, forestall, or remedy certain consequences whose existence or inevitability we may or may not have established to the public's satisfaction.

The dynamic, or structure, underlying these efforts is exactly the same as that underlying the pronouncements of those adversarial folk who predict economic paralysis or the loss of individual liberties as a result of governmental regulation: paint a bloody picture of a negative result, bang the drum furiously, and wrestle the public consciousness and the social fabric into some new configuration. This process is uninspiring and self-limiting, and if we want to build the world to which most of us claim some degree of heart- and soul-felt commitment, we had better come up with something more effective.

Just imagine a great musician trying to contribute effectively to the performance of, say, Beethoven's *Eroica* by riveting his or her attention on *preventing* his or her violin from slipping to the floor, or *forestalling* the conductor's tendency to drink excessively prior to performances, or *repairing* the occasionally defective music stands provided by the management of the hall. It's an absurd image. It does not matter that a firmly held instrument, a sober conductor, and a reliable music stand are all devoutly to be wished by any member of any orchestra. A musician who behaved in this way could be charitably described as neurotic.

Great artists are not first problem solvers; they are first creators, who solve problems secondarily as a necessary and inevitable result of their commitment to producing a remarkable artistic result. The members of a successful orchestra share a deeply rooted common vision (if that is the right word where the product is primarily heard rather than seen). Together they acknowledge their collective errors and momentary limitations, and move on. But the power that moves the orchestra resides first and foremost in its dedication to music, *which it loves and which inspires its members*, not in its ability to correct or avoid mistakes.

It would be foolish to dismiss as accidental, or incidental, the fact that both Mohandas K. Gandhi and Martin Luther King, Jr., were individuals of a deep and abiding spirituality. The type of creativity we are dealing with in such individuals (I occasionally think of it as "deep creativity," though "high creativity" would be equally descriptive)[3] is in truth inseparable from individual spirituality. By "individual spirituality" I mean the substance of personal spirituality, not the label under which that spirituality may exist. A statement attributed to Gandhi in the movie that bears his name captures my perceptions on this subject: addressing a Hindu crowd that does not want him to meet with the Muslim leader Mohammed Ali Jinnah, Gandhi responds, "*I* am a Muslim, and a Hindu, and a Christian, and a Jew — and so are all of you." The spirituality with which I am concerned is one that acknowledges both the limitations of the human ego and the great opportunity of allowing *inspiration* to guide us in the accomplishment of worthwhile ends.

Still, we are given the example of a Gandhi or a King — or a Mother Teresa, an Aung San Suu Kyi, or a Li Lu — not so that we may idolize them for their spirituality or other attributes, and thus keep them at a safe distance, but as both a reminder and a structural model of how any one of *us* might choose to live. (Thoreau commented, "I would not have anyone adopt *my* mode of living on any account; . . . but I would have each one be very careful to find out and pursue *his* own way." The wisdom of his reflection remains current.) The relevance of great lives to each of us lies in a pattern of profoundly successful choices rather than in specific outward forms of behavior. And the sounding of the triangle is as important to a piece of great music as is the playing of the first violin. The greatness of Dr. King is in one sense held aloft by the spirit of Rosa Parks, who on a given day said "enough is enough" and chose to sit at the front of the bus. Individual mission is, well, individual. The willingness of individuals to establish and bear with structural tension, as defined by Robert Fritz, needs to be applied at moments specific to each person.

The great singer Marian Anderson, who saw her primary mission as music but who also became a powerful symbol for all those who believed in civil rights, said that while she deeply respected those who *fought* for justice and other great causes, she was not a fighter by nature. She believed that by following her primary calling and opening herself to God's instruction she had been led into those circumstances which gave her life its greatest impact on the world. That is a rather calm and seemingly undramatic approach to activism, but for Marian Anderson it was dramatically effective.

We need the toughness of the fighter — and the willingness to go the distance — but today the world needs less of the orientation toward combat for combat's sake. We need more Marian Andersons and far fewer would-be John Browns. A major distinction between deeply creative, mission-centered people and those primarily invested in the reactive-responsive orientation described by Robert Fritz lies in the tendency of the latter to think and speak of their efforts in terms of "fight," "struggle," or the equivalent. The former are generally preoccupied with the imagery and language of creating — "shaping," "making," "moulding," "generating," and so on. (One hears the "language of the struggle" in the environmental movement all the time, and the suggestion that there might be a self-fulfilling aspect to this orientation, or at least an unproductive feedback loop, is rarely met with open-mindedly. Attachment to old habits dies hard.) It's true that even highly creative people may lapse into the language of the struggle, but that is not where their hearts lie.

One benchmark for the maturing of Western activism will be the gradual disappearance of "fight language" from both its public and its private pronouncements. Along with it will go melodramatic, apocalyptic images unaccompanied by counter-balancing, powerfully drawn visionary descriptions of the world to come. This change in language and imagery will accompany a deep sense of beauty and of the symphonic in our life and consciousness, while retaining a toughminded willingness to confront forces corrosive to the welfare of humanity and of the earth. It will imply that we have, as a species, begun to seriously entertain the idea that we not only inhabit the spaceship but are endowed with the ability to redesign certain aspects of it — *but only in accordance with those higher laws* which Thoreau implicitly and explicitly illuminated in *Walden* a century and a half ago.

It will also require such entities as Greenpeace to return to and review a core philosophy which embraces nonviolence, and to expand the working definition of that philosophy beyond the boundaries with which many of us have become (relatively) comfortable. For in a very real sense, as I have occasionally if whimsically said (with apologies to John Paul Jones), we have not yet begun *not to fight*.

Chapter Five

The Activism
of the Hologram

Toward the end of my tenure with Greenpeace, the organization vigorously confronted the French government of Jacques
Chirac over its resumption of nuclear testing in the South Pacific. It was an issue of some emotion for us. We had repeatedly
taken strong stands versus one French president or another on
the issue for more than twenty years, seeing our vessels rammed,
seized, or sunk in the process, and suffering the loss of one of our
people at the hands of the French Secret Service in the 1985
sinking of the original *Rainbow Warrior.*

My personal involvement in this last round of confrontations
consisted of three times privately and intensely debating the
French consul general in Los Angeles, in conjunction with
demonstrations outside his office. It was an object lesson in remaining focused on the better nature of an adversary. At one
point, trying to summarize the situation, I wrote to several
colleagues:

> This [consul general] is no hack. His comments on Bos-
> nia, Somalia, and other issues, particularly his comments
> on the situation of children in these and other places and
> some personal statements about his previous career, make
> it plain that he works actively for good causes. He has how-

ever a predictable blind spot where the issue of France's (alleged) security is involved. It illustrates the challenge of inspiring good people to rise to a level of greatness, necessarily putting much at stake in the process.

My concentration on the higher side of the consul general's nature went through some serious lapses in the course of our discussions. There came also an interesting moment when we were joined by actor and activist Martin Sheen, whose debating style is a good deal more robust than mine. The acrimony became sufficiently intense that we were nearly shown the door. But the sharpness on Sheen's side was almost incidental, the external vehicle of his genuine desire to drive home a point for the deeper benefit of his opponent. And as we left the consul general's offices, as if to unconsciously underscore that his intense style truly implied no personal hostility, Sheen said quietly, "He's a good man." My response, delivered with some feeling of regret, was "That's the problem."

The individual with whom we had argued our case was indeed a man of much goodness and considerable integrity. But his goodness — like that of most people — was hemmed in by a code of *behavior* that rendered him incapable of dealing with the situation on its merits. Persuading him to rise above that code — in a sense, to transcend himself — was a challenge beyond our immediate skills.

This situation nonetheless reinforced my perceptions about how to best affect events in the long run, which requires an impact on the deeper structure of things. I accept Gandhi and the Dalai Lama (among others) on this point: when a perception of the potential goodness of your adversary is firmly planted in your consciousness, you are in the position to positively affect that adversary in the long term. And I am emphatically *not* limiting this principle to such cases as the above, where the person you confront is outwardly appealing or attractive. We have to be willing to go beyond interpersonal emotions of all kinds to get at the substantive realities of life. At that level, even though I may experience a complex constellation of sentiments, I am in truth working from an *intention* that is unselfish. I am, in fact, working from love in a form beyond mere sentiment. It is for me an article of faith that this affords me an access into the deep substance of life, where lasting positive change begins.

In *Earth in the Balance*, Al Gore twice makes reference to a model of the relationship of humanity to the world that has great potential power: the model of the hologram. He notes that in the holographic process "every small portion of the photographic plate contains all the visual information necessary to recreate a tiny, faint representation of the entire three-dimensional image," and goes on to analogize that this "resembles the way each individual, like a single small part of a holographic plate, reflects, however faintly, a representation of the sum total of . . . the society of which he or she is a part." Later in the book, he quite eloquently redraws the analogy to embrace deeper, spiritual implications.

It's a model that has struck me ever since I first heard it described by a family member. It's also a model that could be used to far greater effect if those of us who use it stood it on its head once in a while and examined the implications.

If, given the structure of a hologram, one alters the image it projects, every "mini-hologram" it contains must change as well. If you were able to reach into that fascinating, shimmering little three-dimensional picture on your credit card and change it, you would simultaneously be changing the tiny image shown on each minuscule fragment of the thing as well. To have this effect, however, the change you made would have to be in the image itself — not just a scratch on the surface of the material that contains it. Now invert this imaginary exercise and note that *if you could change the image in one small fragment, you would change the entire "parent" hologram.* This is so important that I'm going to say it again: if you alter the image in any fragment of a hologram, you change the whole thing. The profound implication of Gore's analogy is that each one of us who accepts real growth and creative change in her or his life is inevitably transforming society. The catch? The growth and change must take place at a very deep and genuine level: as in the case of your credit card, scratching the surface won't do the job.

At this point I have a disconcerting picture in my mind of thousands of people dissecting their credit cards in a vain attempt to empirically judge the validity of the model. So I ask you to accept the model on its own terms, as a useful hypothesis (even though, as a social and environmental activist, I might be tickled at the subversive shredding of all that plastic). I'm suggesting that the hologram we are working with in our collective life arises from the deepest levels of consciousness. It is affected by the growth of the individual and collective spirit — but by nothing less. If you have the courage (a word originating in the Latin for "heart," as does the related word "core") to enter the domain of spirit and work outward from that point, you have leverage surpassing that of Archimedes. There are no definable limitations on what you can accomplish for society and the world.

I sometimes think that successful activists accept this model of "holographic leverage," more or less unconsciously given the specific individual, as a matter of course. I sometimes think they have to accept it, functionally at least (intellectually, some activists I know might cheerfully argue *against* it), to retain their ability to rise to their everyday challenges. Indeed, at times their mental, emotional, and spiritual well-being may require tacit acceptance of such a model.

An activist like Niaz Dorry — a remarkable, dedicated woman who lived among the people of East Liverpool, Ohio, during one phase of their much-publicized effort to block a hazardous waste incinerator, who has also lived and worked with the fisherfolk of the country, helping to shape a sustainable future for the fishing industry, and who has had greater longevity as a campaigner at Greenpeace than all but a tiny minority — effectively radiates a subliminal message: "We can and will change this for the better, starting now." Without this subtext, accompanied in Niaz's case by a great and evident concern for individuals, the efforts of activists will surely bear minor fruit. It is not just a matter of having an optimistic personality.

Personalities among activists vary considerably: some of my former colleagues, like Campbell Plowden, a decade-long campaigner on the issue of whaling and for several more years in charge of our work on rainforests (and a personal hero of mine), embody the maxim of "We can" with a quietness that sometimes masks the intensity of their efforts. Yet in the course of his career, Campbell performed such exploits as handcuffing himself to the harpoon gun of a Peruvian whaling ship (risking attendant bodily harm) with as much panache as some who were outwardly much more aggressive.

Others, like longtime anti-pesticides campaigner Sandra Marquardt (now with Mothers & Others for a Livable Planet, and experienced at everything from closed-door negotiation to blockading pesticide-laden freighters), or pulp-and-paper campaigner and media liaison Mark Floegel, have carried themselves and their message assertively — and tended to express it very directly. Having at one point been handcuffed to Mark and others in an attempt to block the driveway of the White House, I can state with some conviction that his native style of protest is among the more deeply and physically vigorous I have encountered. What does not appear to me to change, among the successful campaigners, is the degree of faith involved. They *know* they can change things for the better, and they happen to be right.

To revisit the old saw of "Think globally, act locally" in the light of this model is to perceive that every local act is global in effect if it arises from the soul at the moment you perform it. You cannot actually change the hologram by manipulating even large and apparently dramatic areas of its surface. But you can substantively improve the entire work by enhancing the character of its most microscopic fragment at the level where it was created.

I do not know any better summation of the implications of "holographic leverage" than this quotation from Gandhi: "We must be the change we wish to see in the world." The difficulty most people have with this — in Western culture, at least — is that our cultural emphasis on correct behavior translates Gandhi's transpersonal maxim into an intolerable *behavioral* burden on the individual. We persuade ourselves that he means that anyone who wants to improve the world must master every correct behavior in the areas of proposed improvement. The task seems so laughably monumental and so infinite (there being a virtually endless array of correct behaviors associated with any principle) that most people give the entire subject as wide a berth as circumstances will allow them. We suppose there have been a handful of people in humanity's history who accepted the task of learning all the necessary, prescribed behaviors attached to the most critical principles; we call them saints and conveniently isolate them by imagining them to be utterly superior and effectively inimitable. They exist, functionally, apart from our daily lives, our prayers and our reverence — however sincere — notwithstanding. The relief we feel, thus separated (and insulated) from such paragons, is palpable. So do thousands, in the present state of things, initiate the tragedy of escaping from their own innate goodness.

But Gandhi's ultimate intent was not to prescribe behavior; it was to inspire a vision of oneself and the world from which worthy behavior would inevitably arise. The Western tradition of "successful" and "humanistic" behavior, which in America, at least, leans heavily on Puritanical notions of bootstraps and hair shirts, suggests that you have to behave as if you were committed before you can create or establish a commitment. This is fallacious. The biblical injunction is *first* to have faith, and if you find you don't have it, only secondly — as a sort of Graceful fallback position — to act *as if* you had it, in which case "faith will be given to you." To reverse these priorities is, in a sense, to arrogantly demand of the tail that it wag the dog.

Gandhi or Dr. King, or Elizabeth of Hungary or Jefferson or Joan of Arc, or Tesla or Edison, for that matter, did not behave as they did because they were *trying* to commit themselves; they committed themselves first and allowed the opportunity and the inspiration for successful behaviors to come to them. And when inspiration and opportunity came, they embraced them — which does not mean, by the way, that the experience was necessarily either comfortable or uncomfortable, but just that each had positioned himself or herself to appreciate and take advantage of the chance to further a worthy cause. Discomfort in and of itself is no final indicator of virtue. "Creative discomfort," the sort of stress which *is* a reliable indicator, arises from the inherent challenge of a worthy goal, not from self-denial practiced for its own sake.

People who have actually committed themselves freely to a worthy goal to the point where discomfort and stress cannot undermine them ultimately find — or *create* — behaviors that embody their commitment. On some level activists know this; that is why many are constantly nagged by the sense that there must be new, superior, and yet more radical ways to get their messages across. (They might for a start try granting themselves — individually and collectively, and within the boundaries of their guiding philosophies — greater tolerance of apparent "failure," as a healthy means of promoting long-term success. If it does not do to take Grace for granted, neither can it be healthy, wise, or humble to close off the avenues by which Grace appears.)

An ill-kept secret of the great agents of improvement in the world has been their functional acceptance of the idea that *all limitations on our creativity are finally self-imposed.* It often requires some act of great commitment before a person's eyes are opened to this principle. Most self-imposed limitations arise from the unconscious act — an act, nonetheless — of accepting the near-universal assumption that we are *all* limited. This makes the process very difficult to identify. The experience of recognizing and then going beyond the limitations that society accepts as self-evident is a little like identifying, naming, rejecting, and escaping from quicksand after having been born into the stuff, raised by and among millions of others who aren't even conscious of its existence, and regularly and constantly being bombarded with implicit and deliberate messages that "This Is Just The Way Things Are." Nevertheless, some do identify the trap and some have always managed to escape from it. Their model of reality is distinctly different from the models of those who, however unconsciously, *choose* to coexist passively with the mud.

Just for a moment — as much for the fun of it as for serious effect — close your eyes and imagine that there are no limitations *of any kind* on your ability to do good in the world. Now imagine further that there is a foolproof mechanism in place which guarantees that even if you choose your goals with imperfect wisdom, your good intentions will be turned to great ends. Notice what experience of freedom this brings. If you had such unlimited power to make the world better, where would you begin? What cause sways your heart?

Without ignoring the reality that time, as Tennessee Williams put it, "lives in the world with us," and transforming the world does *take* time, or the fact that creating also entails hard work, the point is that you *do* have such unlimited creative power — and the freedom to use it.

Chapter Six

New Model, New Map

As most people are aware, Greenpeace first became prominent in the international press — and widely popular — in the mid-seventies, when it took up the cause of saving the great whale species. (Many people think this was the group's first campaign. It wasn't: the organization had been active on the issue of nuclear weapons testing since its founding in 1971.) Few people, however, are aware of the constellation of circumstances that surrounded the success of Greenpeace's initial voyage on behalf of the whales, even though it has been eloquently described in at least two excellent books that I know of, Robert Hunter's *Warriors of the Rainbow* (1979) and Rex Weyler's later *Song of the Whale.*[1]

The facts are these. After a great deal of diligent and remarkable legwork on the part of Paul Spong — the scientist who persuaded Greenpeace to take up the whales' cause — the approximate location of the Russian whaling fleet in the early summer of 1975 was discovered.[2] But actually finding even so substantial an entity as a whaling fleet on the open ocean is not a casual task, even when you know what part of the Pacific to search. This is all the more true when you are in an ancient fishing boat — the *Phyllis Cormack*, an old standby chartered once again for this voyage and temporarily renamed the *Greenpeace V.* The crew did the best they could, even tracking the fleet well enough that they could occasionally hear its radio chatter. But after many days of searching they had never made physical contact.

At a significant juncture the helm fell to a crew member of a musical and mystical bent. No left-brained slave to either maritime or social conventions, Melville Gregory (manning the helm au naturel that evening in both a literal and a figurative sense) elected to steer toward the moon rather than follow the course prescribed. This earned him the wrath of the captain and a reprieve from duty at the helm, putatively for the remainder of the voyage. But as fortune, fate, or destiny would have it, Mel Gregory was afforded another chance to prove his mettle. Which indeed he did, by once more utterly discarding the prescriptions of his nautical betters and steering this time toward a rainbow, an omen of curious significance in the history of Greenpeace. With this new dereliction, given the temperament of the boat's skipper, Gregory risked such dramatic retribution as keelhauling. But the captain had chosen precisely that moment to take a nap. "Thirty minutes later," records Robert Hunter, who was aboard the *Greenpeace V,* "the Russian whaling fleet appeared on the horizon — dead ahead."

As far as I know, history does not report whether Mel Gregory then laid claim to absolute intuitive foreknowledge or simply took this astonishing outcome in his mystical stride. What is clear in hindsight is that since the Greenpeace vessel was down to its last day or two of fuel (and the International Whaling Commission meeting the group sought to influence, a focus for the media, was nearing an end), Greenpeace's popular success — which grew directly out of film footage of its subsequent confrontation with the Russians that summer — hinged on the anarchic navigational choices made by one seemingly irrational crew member.

A second example of such Graceful happenstance or amendment follows hard on the first. This is because the film footage of Greenpeacers standing in a tiny inflatable motorboat directly in the path of a Russian harpoon, which missed them by the narrowest of margins, was a rational impossibility. The cameraman who took it had definitively ascertained that his camera battery was quite dead. In an act of either divine foolishness or paradigmatic faith and with no conscious hope of success, he aimed the camera anyway and pushed the button on the thing an instant before the Russians chose to fire their harpoon.

For a few magnificent seconds the camera sprang to life, catching the firing, the trajectory, the activists in their tiny, bobbing craft, and the ultimate explosion of the harpoon in the whale at which the Russians had been aiming. At precisely that point the battery gave up and no amount of coaxing would persuade it to offer further heroics. Caught on film was exactly the amount of drama sufficient to illustrate the nature of the Greenpeace campaign, the organization's tactics, and the lengths to which its members would go — risking their lives — in pursuit of a worthy aim.

Interestingly, neither of the above instances of synchronicity or Grace are so much as mentioned in the officially sanctioned 1989 volume *The Greenpeace Story.* Ostensibly because the Greenpeace of today feels anxious about the implications of using the language of "alternative culture," public mention of such unique circumstances, or patterns of circumstances, are rare indeed. Beneath the concern with public image there lies a considerable discomfort with discussion of those values in the group's work that are spiritual, and with the limited vocabulary which seems available for such discussion. And yet there is broad acceptance among Greenpeace staff that the work is quintessentially spiritual, though definitions of what is meant by the term vary.

It is not my intent here, however taken I may be with the concept, to make a case for divine or otherworldly intervention in such events as those aboard the *Greenpeace V,* although that sort of claim has been made often enough in activist movements and out of them. What I am after here is a conclusion which is purely clinical: I am suggesting that there is that in the *structure* of reality which transcends the perceptive abilities of the left brain, and I am suggesting that we may position ourselves to engage this part of reality by taking worthwhile risks on behalf of a worthy cause.

Within the organization they helped to birth, the events above are often lightly dismissed as "Greenpeace karma." This casualness can mask an unwillingness to acknowledge the depth of the phenomenon. There is a certain fear of fully acknowledging that there are greater forces at work than the initiative and cleverness of individuals. An open willingness to examine events from a larger, clinical, structure-based perspective, like that offered in the work of Robert Fritz and some others, could afford Greenpeace and all of us a clearer definition of our mission, a greater sense of the latitude we have for experimentation (and even apparent failure in the short term), and a very useful experience of humility about our place in the greater scheme of things.

If we are to deal honestly with the implications of synchronous and serendipitous events like the blessed helmsmanship of Melville Gregory and the astonishing counterpoint furnished by *Greenpeace V* cameraman Fred Easton, we need to expand our individual and collective maps of reality to embrace the territories from which such events arise.

In the spirit of the exercise at the end of the preceding chapter, you might enjoy taking a moment at this point to close your eyes and imagine yourself at the helm of the *Greenpeace V* at the auspicious and critical moments when the moon and the rainbow appeared. (Au naturel or not, as you prefer.) Given the present state of your creative consciousness, might you have been aware of the instinct (or intuition) to "throw away the map," and steer the vessel on an inspired course? If you think you might have been *aware* of the intuition, do you think you would have followed it? It's not a judgment of right or wrong I'm suggesting here, by the way, but an internal reality check. In fact, relatively few people in this culture are consistently open to genuine inspiration, or sturdy enough in their perceptions that they will allow inspiration to guide them once they let it through the door.

Western culture (leaning heavily on "logical" perceptions generally assigned to the left brain) likes to think of reality as proceeding in straight lines. Despite recent developments at the frontiers of science — which has at least *begun* to accept the idea that a linear model of reality has severe limitations — most of us are still brought up to think of life as rather like a pool table, on whose surface one thing is manipulated into propelling something else to strike another, which hits a final object and propels it into a desired location. Most Westerners' mental (and emotional!) processes are still dominated by an assumption that reality is a mechanical business of cause and effect.

But, in the words of Ira Gershwin, "it ain't necessarily so," and creative people generally understand that. The genuinely creative individual's universe embraces the straight lines of cause and effect but expands continuously beyond them. It allows, without necessarily requiring a full explanation of the phenomenon, for some relation to exist between two (or more) events that cannot be rationally connected. The working hypothesis that seemingly unrelated events may, on some level, be quite intimately related or *associated* is one of the most powerful tools available to people who want to facilitate the evolution of humanity and the planet. To borrow somewhat crudely from the pool table analogy, if you can get the eight ball in the corner pocket and win the game (without cheating, of course), do you really care exactly how it gets in there?

In pool there are certain agreed-upon rules of the game that forbid many means of getting a given ball into a given pocket. Even in as rigidly governed a case as this, however, there is some latitude left for the unexpected. If, for instance, you were attempting to sink the aforementioned eight ball in a critical game in, say, Las Vegas, and a small fly distracted you just as you made the shot; and if, just as it appeared that the cue ball would spin fractionally north of its desired trajectory, the Nevada desert chose to manifest the implications of plate tectonics by shifting ever so slightly beneath the pool hall; and if one effect of this exciting evidence of the fluidity of the terrestrial surface just happened to be that the cue ball corrected itself southward, striking the eight ball squarely and dumping it into the specified receptacle, you would win just as legally as if you had made a flawless linear shot under more conventional circumstances. The unanswerable question (which creators do not necessarily think has to be answered) is, Was the relationship between me, the fly, the earthquake, and the eight ball just one of coincidence?

The classic, literal — and geographical — example of the limitations of linear thinking in environmental matters is the diversion of Florida's Kissimmee River, which carries water toward the Everglades, by the Army Corps of Engineers. Ostensibly to help alleviate property damage associated with the river's periodic flooding, the Corps in the 1960s turned a meandering, seemingly random watercourse into a liquid highway running straight as an Arizona interstate from Lake Kissimmee to Lake Okeechobee. The result was a stunningly efficient system of pollution drainage — of chemicals coming largely from agricultural land abutting the river — which brought about the near-death of both Lake Okeechobee and much of the native character of the state of Florida. Forty years later, the straight lines of the Corps' C-38 canal are a pathetic testimony to the inadequacy of human cleverness, and to the wisdom manifested in the complex yet wonderfully balanced systems of nature. Thanks primarily to the dauntless efforts of the late, great Marjory Stoneman Douglas, and her successors, the Corps is now busy reversing, or trying to reverse, its old reconstruction. It has also been required to review the impact of its other canals, running east and southeast from Lake Okeechobee to the ocean.

The short-term "payoff" of holding rigidly to a linear model of things, of course, is that the individual and collective human ego is able to maintain the illusion that it is in control. That maintaining this illusion routinely requires a denial of many aspects of character (spirituality; intuition; compassion) that are essential to being fully human has not, historically, been a sufficient disincentive. That it has required massive manipulation of events and of the physical planet, and an almost unimaginable waste of both psychic and physical energy, has also been insufficiently offputting to motivate our species to relinquish this illusion. But the time is at hand when our collective somnambulence threatens to propel us into a bracing encounter with the larger reality.

The essence of action based on linear thinking is that it tends to force into comfortingly straight lines something that by nature wants to run a less rationally predictable course. The irony is that when a larger picture of reality is taken into account, a visionary approach, which allows for the *associative* nature of things — the tendency of events to associate with one another in unpredictable ways — always yields a more direct, effective means of accomplishing the most important goals. The route the river wants to take is ultimately better not just for the river, but for the human beings its diversion was supposed to benefit.[3]

I do not say that a given visibly linear path through a given part of reality is inevitably doomed to failure. My point is that a linear orientation is inherently limited, not that it is incapable of generating certain useful results. More broadly, I am suggesting that linear reality is a subcategory of associative reality. And a map of associative reality thus yields a far more complete picture of the world than does a map that sees reality as strictly linear, because it makes allowance for linear connections between many things while leaving possibilities for other relationships open.

Intuition — *real* intuition, not "gut feeling" or other pseudo-experience — is an inborn, if quiescent, human trait which affords an access into those other relationships. We all have it, though few of us allow it much play in our lives. An extraordinary quantity of psychic energy has thus necessarily been expended by this culture, however unconsciously, in holding its collective intuitive perception at bay. But today we live in a time when the greatest mathematicians and astrophysicists openly acknowledge a reality that transcends the five usual senses. In a world where science has been forced, even while operating according to its own rational tenets, to acknowledge the likelihood that reality consists not of a mere three dimensions, but of nine — or thirteen, or twenty-six — the suppression of those perceptive abilities which permit an *awareness* of a more complete picture becomes an increasingly dicey proposition.[4] It is a little like robbing oneself of depth perception by covering one eye while attempting to drive at full speed through midtown Manhattan at rush hour. Yes, a great driver might survive the trip, but would the ego boost really be worth the risk — not to mention the aggravation?

It cedes nothing to the creationists (whose beautiful mythology and metaphors are of another time) to point out that science is giving us the mythology of today. Great scientists such as Einstein, who said that he wanted "to know God's thoughts," have sometimes shared the perception that their best theories were no more literal or absolute than great poetry. What is intriguing about contemporary science is that it is now offering conclusions which parallel, or perhaps I should say echo, thousands of years of spiritual tradition.[5] The idea that we do share an existence in multiple, invisible dimensions is the modern acknowledgment that our spiritual nature is real — and that we should tread gently, for we affect more than we know, or allow ourselves to know.

I am sympathetic to creationist sentiments to the extent that I do not think science, broadly speaking, has yet gone near the core of what religion is about — nor is it likely to do so in the near term. God, as Robert Frost brilliantly put it in "A Masque of Reason," retains as his "forte" "truth / Or metaphysics, long the world's reproach / For standing still in one place true forever; / While science goes self-superseding on." But I'm quite willing to borrow from the limited mythology of science when it helps me make an important point — or reinforces my own sense of what spirituality means.

As an activist, I am practically concerned with developing that view of reality, whether derived from religion, science, or any other useful source, which best enables me to creatively and constructively affect the course of events. If (as I am happy to believe) prayer will do it, I'm for it. If meditation will work to the end of nurturing a healthier world, I'll do some of that. And if an exploration of seemingly nonrational, intuitive areas of human perception has the slightest chance of affording useful insights into how we can restore the Garden, then you can sign me up.

The critical issue — for anyone with a real commitment to living a meaningful life and creating a workable society — is being alert to a tendency to take an obvious, comforting, linear route that will satisfy superficial concerns *even when it does so at the expense of more important ones.* A given "rational," linear formula might even work pretty well ninety-nine times out of a hundred. The truly creative individual is the one who can intuitively and accurately identify that hundredth occasion when the formula will *not* work and indeed may yield results that are, especially in the long-term, disastrous. Such an individual is inherently involved in a form of activism — because she or he refuses to maintain a given psychological comfort level at the expense of genuine progress.

Chapter Seven

Catch a Standing Wave

In the last few years I have been intrigued to observe a transition within Greenpeace, most tangibly evidenced in some of its European offices and in Australia. Starting with Greenpeace Germany's sponsorship of a refrigeration technology that is entirely "ozone-friendly" (known as "greenfreeze"), continuing with Greenpeace Australia's early role in designing an ecologically advanced Olympic Village for the games of the year 2000, and extending to the European unveiling of a prototype superfuel-efficient car, the group has increasingly demonstrated an interest in going well beyond its traditional image as protester against the status quo. These forays in design have earned for the organization some recognition and leverage as a proactive force. True, much of the language being used in this process is the language of "solutions," but at its best the movement toward proactivity has gone beyond mere problem solving. It shows some promise of being a movement toward genuine creativity rather than just an expansion of the concept of putting fingers into eroding dikes.

In the United States, the 25,000-mile tour in 1994 of our solar-photovoltaic generator, the *Cyrus* (a converted tractor-trailer truck which, among other things, powered the eco-village at Woodstock), was an interesting development. Traveling with the *Cyrus* — which I did through much of the Midwest, as a sort of pinch-hitter for ailing campaigners, and also in Southern California — afforded a unique and happy opportunity to drive up to people's homes in a functional piece of the future. It gave us the chance to say, for a change, "Here is a tangible part of what works," as opposed to "Here's what's broken." This kind of investment of time and skills is a long-term one and peculiarly important. The lives of the people of the Altgeld Gardens housing project, on the southeast side of Chicago, are not measurably altered by two days' exposure to the *Cyrus* (which we used there to power the public address system for a community rally and a talent contest), but that does not diminish the importance of Greenpeace being there. The visionary needs to spend time wherever the vision is needed.

One aspect of the approach symbolized by the *Cyrus* and Greenpeace's other ventures in the area of creative design is the championing of an activism that is experimental. As important as any tangible results is the spirit behind them, which relishes the opportunity to create new patterns in the world as much as it relishes new products or processes.[1] It is Gandhi's principle again: "We must be the change we wish to see in the world." If you want to get down deep enough into things to make lasting positive change, you must work, as the hologram model suggests, at the level where such patterns begin. Let go of some old forms, take the risk of proposing some very new ones — and embody them in your own individual or institutional life.

In his writing and lecturing on the creative nature of human consciousness, Deepak Chopra regularly refers to the "field of all possibilities" from which our reality emerges. The reality we experience, he says, is drawn to us by the activity of our individual consciousness, according to our degree of mastery of the laws by which consciousness operates. As a physician trained in both Eastern and Western medicine, he is particularly effective in articulating the implications of this situation for the well-being of our bodies.

One of his essential points has to do with the recognition and improvement of patterns deeply set in our consciousness. While the body changes utterly as cells replace themselves, a given physical condition, healthy or unhealthy, may remain — long outlasting the cells that gave rise to it. From the perspective of Eastern medical tradition, this is indicative of the persistence of a disturbance in the consciousness of the patient. (Needless to say, Western medicine is still groping toward this conclusion, just as it is still groping toward some understanding and acceptance of the implications of acupuncture, meditation — which it has now reinvented in the form of Dr. Herbert Benson's "relaxation response" — and other alien disciplines.) When I first heard Dr. Chopra raise this point, it reminded me of a recurrent image I had studied years ago in college: the "standing wave" metaphor found in various guises in the poetry of Robert Frost, and most fully articulated in the great poem "West-running Brook."

As any experienced canoeist or kayaker knows, a standing wave is an illusory phenomenon, found where flowing water strikes a submerged object and, at the surface, turns back upon itself. The water itself continues to flow forward, but the wave-*form* appears stationary. Frost thoughtfully imagined it as "the tribute of the current to the source," and drew from it an extraordinary and moving analog of human existence. In the case of Deepak Chopra's investigation of the relationship between our consciousness and our health, the image has practical applications that relate to the image of the hologram.

If one thinks of a given physical condition as a standing waveform which may persist, apparently static, even while the dynamic processes of the body continue on within and around it, one can understand Dr. Chopra's comments on the mastery of creative consciousness as suggesting how we may affect the wave pattern itself — rather than just treating symptoms manifested as a consequence of that underlying pattern. This is another way of stating the requirement that to affect the hologram you must work at the level of the image itself, not just on the level of the material in which it is embedded: you cannot permanently alter the waveform just by splashing about in the water, you must create a new structure in the streambed.

It is a leap, but not an unmanageable one for the imaginative soul, from Chopra's model of human health to a "standing wave" model for the health of the planet. For if we shape the patterns in our individual consciousness which manifest themselves in physical health or disease, so do we shape the patterns in our collective consciousness which are manifest in the health or illness of our cultures and, finally, of the earth as a whole. In Chopra's holistic model, mastery of one's individual well-being hinges on one's ability to enter that "field of all possibilities" and reemerge carrying within one's consciousness the seeds of improved health. Mastery of the process by which our uniquely gifted species affects the well-being of earth will, in this model, require a similar journey — preferably by the many.

The coexistence of the hologram concept and standing wave metaphor should underscore the rather important point that each is a *model for*, not some ultimate description of, the mechanics of reality. The power of the best models and metaphors rests in their timely existence as great suggestions of the possibilities of life and the world, not as final answers. This is as true of the theorems of scientists as it is of the imagery of poets, though Western science would sometime prefer to overlook or deny the fact. In physics, a Newton is always tipped by an Einstein, who is subject to revision (at the least) by a Hawking. In metaphysics, even though its author had signed off from the Christian church, Thoreau's exploration of higher laws is in part a revisitation of the Bible, of which he justly complained that "some old poet's grand imagination is imposed on us as adamantine, everlasting truth, and God's own word!"

The distinction between genuine or creative control of events and the sham, manipulative control characteristic of the reactive-responsive approach to life depends greatly on one's ability to regard life as Thoreau recommended, as an experiment. This Thoreauvian approach runs significantly counter to the problem-solving, answer-addicted mentality that pervades our culture and now affects — or infects — activists just as potently, with rare exceptions, as it affects the captains, corporals, *et al.*, of industry and government. The latter orientation worships, unconsciously for the most part, at the altar of conflict. The "high" that most people associate with what passes for creativity consists largely of the exultation of the ego at having attacked, wrestled with, and conquered an obstacle. But that is precisely the mindset — the pattern — which has nearly destroyed our culture's relationship to the natural world, the domination and manipulation of which has effectively preoccupied our collective consciousness to the exclusion of anything but the most occasional, and usually sentimental, appreciation of nature's actual beauty and worth. The same mindset has also limited the vast majority of human relationships, whether between individuals or nations, whether in family life or commerce, public service or international diplomacy, to wistful shadows of what they might have been.

The true experimental consciousness cares only incidentally about solutions to life's problems: it wants first to coexist in creative interaction with ever larger and more rewarding questions. It is interested in nearly everything and fascinated by nothing. It understands that necessary information, explanations, and means are in truth *invited into existence* — not forcibly extracted from life — by its own open-ended and open-minded willingness to live with an experience of insecurity. (Deepak Chopra talks of "cultivating uncertainty" in the life process.) The real reward of creativity, the part of the "high" that is genuine, comes from the unselfish alignment of individual consciousness with benevolent creative forces larger than the mind operating in allegedly splendid isolation. It suggests a state nearer to exaltation than exultation.

This experiment-oriented approach to life advanced by Thoreau implies an attitude recommended in Zen Buddhism, what might be called the orientation of the perpetual novice. As that phrase suggests, this is an attitude, if not entirely of humility as the West pictures it, at least of constant curiosity and perhaps surprise about how much one does not yet know. It requires one to constantly revisit the notion that one is, after all, only a beginner at virtually everything because the amount remaining to be learned about everything perpetually dwarfs the amount one already (ostensibly) knows.

Just as an exercise, examine your personal sense of expertise. In what areas do you consider yourself an expert? Now, imagine functioning in those areas as if you were a complete novice. Would you be able to fully accept happy results in those areas of your life and work if you *didn't* feel like an expert, if your ego didn't feel "in control" of the process? Your (truthful) answer will tell you much about your present status: are you a creator, or are you (thus far) a problem solver? There's a difference — which doesn't make it "wrong" to be a problem solver, just less powerful in the long term. That problem-solving orientation, based in the largely unconscious experience of conflict as entertainment, is tied to the ego's quest for temporary satisfaction, usually at the expense of long-term fulfillment. A significant number of people who believe themselves to be immensely creative are actually stuck in a limited process of solving preexisting problems. To be fair, some people who may appear to be problem solvers — and even think of themselves as such — are actually creators.

People with a beginner's orientation are often more creative than established "authorities" because they haven't learned *formulas* for success, so they often avoid the trap of manipulating the surface of the "reality hologram," or the "standing wave," and have access to the deeper stuff of life. And in my model of things, the beginner's orientation also has this singular advantage: it positions one to be the beneficiary of Beginner's Luck.

Part of the reason I here capitalize that last phrase is that it happens to be the title of one of the more memorable plays I have ever seen, a wonderful piece based on the biblical story of Saul and David. It was written by a former colleague of mine in the Boston theatre community, Jon Lipsky. I saw this work nearly twenty years ago, but remember vividly its presentation of Saul as the embattled veteran who is overtaken by a new order whose nature and inevitability he is simply unprepared to grasp. On a human level, the play evoked sympathy for the character of a powerful leader who is overtaken by the transformation of the world he inhabits. On other levels — including that of the unique, stylized performance given by the actors of the Reality Theater, at that time arguably Boston's best troupe — the work had the power to vigorously mobilize an audience's spirit behind the sense that change and even transformation are inevitable, and had much better be met head-on than evaded, resisted, or denied. It was this experience of being almost bodily lifted out of my seat by the play, thrown into an experience of disorientation from comfortable and familiar realities and then set back down the wiser in my chair, that has kept that evening of theatre alive in my memory.

I suspect that the current age of the world is one in which that experience of "creative disorientation" is going to be recreated for virtually everybody, on a grand scale in real life. Given that premise, it would seem like an intelligent idea to orient oneself toward the world rather more along the lines of a David than a Saul. Among activists of my acquaintance, such reorientation is only partly in evidence. I hope the phenomenon will expand. For the orientation of the perpetual novice, and the openness to inspiration that accompanies it (along with the occasional experience of beginner's luck), have much to recommend them.

If you are willing to take the rather bold step of seeing yourself as a novice — if you are even able to conceive that such a step *might be fun* to take — you are probably one of those people who is positively affecting the "standing wave" pattern for this cul-

ture, and for humankind. To further your personal commitment, you will almost certainly pay ever-deepening attention to
your personal vision for your life and that of this work of art we
call Earth. You will also find that planting the seeds of hope and
vision in the hearts of others is incalculably important in your
work.

Bringing forward something tangible and demonstrable
from the "field of all possibilities" can put activists in the driver's seat of this culture in a way that nothing else can. To bring
your vision into reality, you will need to act in accordance with
the principles that vision embraces. And one of the skills you
will need to ensure that both your goals and the actions you take
toward those goals are well chosen — and that you, like the ethical physician, "do no harm" — is intuition.

Chapter Eight

Activism and Intuition

The first Greenpeace "direct action" in which I took a serious part in the United States was near Niagara Falls. Quite near, in fact: it involved placing a (regrettably temporary) steel cap over a discharge pipe in the Niagara River at a facility now owned by Occidental Chemical, the former Hooker Chemical plant of Love Canal fame. This old and broken pipe ran through one of the many less famous dumping areas along the river, and years after the furor over Love Canal had died down, it continued to serve as an unintended collector and conduit for lethal wastes. It opened into the river about two miles above the falls and was significantly responsible for the fact that the spray from the falls had become technically hazardous to human health by the standards of the Environmental Protection Agency. At its mouth the Ontario Environment Ministry found, among other organochlorinated artifacts, dramatic concentrations of the banned pesticide Mirex.

Greenpeace had plugged the pipe once before, drawing a degree of publicity, during a tour of the Great Lakes basin in 1985. We returned to the site in May of 1988 for the simple reason that nothing had changed. A sapling the group had planted near the pipe in 1985 now stood lifeless above the outfall. Occidental, quicker to respond to the "threat" posed by nonviolent activists than to that posed to the public by the lethal chemicals there, had placed a grating at the mouth of the pipe so that plugs could no longer be inserted. Thus on our return we were required to construct a massive metal cap rather than a simpler, wood-and-inner-tubing plug.

During the several days surrounding this return visit, we were hosted on nearby Grand Island by a small local church composed entirely of activists who were veterans of the citizen action begun at Love Canal. The night before our pipe plugging took place, I stayed up until all hours in the cabin they made available to us, creating a stencil and painting "GREEN-PEACE" on the cap, remedying an oversight that might have undermined the impact of television coverage of the next day's events. I recall pretty well the mixed constellation of emotions and sensations as I worked, ranging from enjoyment of the minor artistic process to intense stress and a feeling of physical exhaustion.

Fear was also a highly perceptible element in the mix. I was thirty-eight years old, and though I had recently been in the thick of a Canadian protest at a paper mill near the St. Lawrence River, and had been chased through the woods of upstate New York by security guards while photographing a joint U.S.-Canadian action, this was the first time I was to face arrest. This would presumably be preceded by direct confrontation with more private security guards, who are notoriously unpredictable in their response to protesters. And I would be contending with all this while standing *in* the Niagara River, at a point where it is quite possible to get swept into the current, while my companions and I wrestled with a two-hundred-pound chunk of steel and attempted to place it over a pipe which was disgorging several score of gallons per minute of toxic discharge, bathing us in poison for as long as we remained there. Notwithstanding our expensive but incomplete "toxics suits," the experience promised to be (and the anticipation alone was), as Thoreau commented of his night in jail, "novel and interesting enough."

So my feelings and sensations were, as I say, diverse. Nonetheless, I was aware that a level of my consciousness I had come largely to trust cast the outcome in a favorable light. It was not (in this case) so much an inner voice as it was a generalized sense of well-being, or at least of well-*doing*: this was where I was supposed to be and there were currents in the stream of circumstance which would in the end prove supportive of our efforts. This sensation was not emotional in quality but *intuitive*, as I had been specifically trained to call it during some intense studies of creativity and related phenomena. I was glad to have made its acquaintance. I was also, as you may understand, surpassingly interested to see how events might prove it out.

The next morning started rather oddly. When we arrived at the outfall we found that Occidental had anticipated us and stationed a guard at the pipe. Curiously, however, he made no move to interfere with us, but in fact stepped aside from the riverbank; as he did so, we were astonished to hear him say, "Do what you have to do." We were cautiously pleased to oblige. Three of us lugged the great steel plate down the bank and lowered it and ourselves into the water. There followed a period of intense activity on our part, during which we managed to grapple the plate to Occidental's protective grating by means of a combination of hooks and bolts.

Growing attention to our efforts also followed, on the part of both Occidental's security guards — one of whom now sat astride the concrete flange of the outfall and thrust a booted foot

onto the shoulder of one of my companions below — and the local media and the local and New York state police (who, to their
credit, warned this new security guard to place his foot elsewhere or risk an assault charge). In the midst of all this, between
the half-blind gropings and periodic submergences necessary
to attach the cap to the steel grating, my other colleague mur-
mured thoughtfully in my direction, "Why don't you be our
spokesman?"

The ultimate result of this nomination was that I had my first
chance to serve as "point person" in negotiation with the authorities, and to subsequently address a few remarks to the
press. Under the circumstances I did not feel unduly flattered by
these opportunities, as I was more or less preoccupied with a)
my survival and b) staying at the outfall as long as possible, to
give the protest some weight. Later it occurred to me what value
this appointment had, both educationally and as a sort of professional credential, and I felt grateful to my companions for
electing me as their mouthpiece.

In the event, as we had supposed, Occidental demanded our
arrest for trespassing on their property (we were), and our deliberate delay in exiting the river nearly cost us a technical New
York State felony charge of resisting arrest. Interestingly, the
state police captain who ordered us out of the water was reluc-
tant to the point of apology about the latter charge, which was
eventually dropped. It was a harbinger of good things to come.

We were bailed out of jail by Greenpeace and ordered to return after several weeks' time to appear before a judge. As often
happens, we were represented by a supportive local attorney
who offered his services pro bono and with evident enthusiasm
for our cause. That was another good sign. On the appointed day

we arrived at the courthouse and learned that of two possible judges, our case was to be heard by the one our counsel thought more likely to be sympathetic. How right he was we would shortly discover.

As we had pled guilty to the remaining misdemeanor charge of trespass, we knew that while there was some possibility of a brief jail term, the most likely outcome was a fine. The amount of such a fine would be largely at the discretion of the judge. We had more or less resigned ourselves to the idea that we would have to cough up something, despite our heartfelt conviction that we had played both a useful and an honorable role. The fine might be several hundreds of dollars, or worse. Like all Greenpeace expenditures, it would ultimately come out of the pool of donations from individuals who support our work, and it would cut into the funds available for our other efforts in the Great Lakes that year. We thus went before the bench with a degree of both trepidation and defensiveness, which made the judge's opening comments that much more startling and encouraging.

Looking up from the paperwork in front of him, he peered at us over the bench and said reflectively, "You're the people from Greenpeace. I like what you do." He paused thoughtfully for a brief second and added, "I'm not sure I always like the *way* that you do it . . ." Here he paused again and seemed to grope for words.

"But I know your heart's in the right place."

We were sufficiently astounded by these remarks to be at a loss for response, which may have been all to the good. After one or two more brief comments, and after assuring himself that we were each sufficiently *compos mentis* to understand what he was about, the judge informed us that there would be no jail time, that there would further be no fine, and that, in short, he was issuing a conditional release — meaning that if we "behaved ourselves" for the next twelve months in New York State, the arrest would be removed from our records. And there was that in his manner which suggested that if it were up to him and if the law did not require this minimum response (since we had, after all, pled guilty to the trespass charge), he would just as soon turn us loose to continue and expand upon the collective *mis*behavior that had brought us before him in the first place.

It was, especially for a novice in the areas of arrest, trial, and justice, a wondrous and gratifying moment. Notwithstanding his prescient comment that this judge would likely be more lenient than the other one available, our lawyer was stunned. We looked at one another as if to assure ourselves that we had all heard the same sentence pronounced, and in joy and some degree of disbelief we gathered our wits sufficiently to leave the courtroom. Thereafter we found means of extensive celebration.

And I thought about that sensation of well-being or welldoing which had persisted even through my night fears in the cabin on Grand Island.

Everyone has moments of general or specific foreknowledge not explainable on the basis of logical precalculation, even at an unconscious level. The difficulty is that the area of consciousness involved is often very hard to isolate or to identify as uniquely valuable. When I hear people say, after some more or less dramatic occurrence, "I *knew* that would happen," I generally show them the respect of taking them at their word. The problem (for them) is that *prior* to the event, they also knew — or felt or thought they knew, or greatly suspected — a number of other outcomes as well. Other sensations, other feelings, and other voices came between them and an actual foreseeing of events.

But true intuition, though cheapened by the mindless melodramatization of "psychic phenomena" in this culture, is as much a part of the human equipment as eyes, ears, or the senses of touch and taste and smell. Curiously, when a person claims to have excellent eyesight we do not expect him or her to then prove infallible in matters hyper-opic, but when the same individual claims to be intuitive or hyperperceptive, the culture generally applies a standard of absolute rigor. Since few people are trained or even encouraged from an early age to explore, develop, or trust such an inner faculty, this cultural response is somewhat like punishing an infant for the inability to read road signs. And that, alas, is a situation which will persist until a very large number of people understand how important it is that the culture's orientation change, demand that change, and significantly preoccupy themselves even *before* the change with learning to hear their own inner wisdom, without self-delusion, above the din of lesser voices in their consciousness.

Ironically, those most successful in fields ostensibly based on principles of logic and rationality, such as business and science, will often admit that they have made many of their best decisions from something other than rational foreknowledge. Reliance on this "something other" involves accepting the inclination of some kind of inner gyroscope. A classic example of both this phenomenon and the success of the beginner's orientation is noted in a January 1996 issue of the journal *Science*. It seems that a safe, simple, cheap means of converting stockpiles of banned chlorofluorocarbons into salt and sodium fluoride was discovered by a Yale graduate student, who used for this process a chemical (sodium oxalate) found in rhubarb leaves. The professor working with him acknowledged that few experts would ever have considered such a "surprising" and "unassuming" process; the graduate student, Juan Burdeniuc, called his discovery a matter of "chemical intuition."

Mr. Burdeniuc probably specified "intuition" correctly. However, the range of stunningly imprecise terms used by others to describe such a faculty — from "gut feeling" to "business instinct" to "a feel for the road" — is impressive. Generally speaking, the inner advice that proves accurate is not based in emotion, does not originate in the abdominal region (where it may or may not subsequently register), and has little to do with highway travel. Again, it usually comes in the form of a distinct sensation that is *not* an emotion but which has a clear impact — strongly encouraging or significantly foreboding — and may have its source, if a location can be specified at all, throughout the region between "head" and "heart." And it is actual perception, not unconscious prejudice dressed self-importantly in new clothes.

This is a vital distinction. The words "intuitive" and, more especially, "counterintuitive" have lately come into somewhat common use in a way which wholly distorts their meaning. I have heard some scientists and a number of journalists, in reporting scientific advances, describe certain conclusions as "counterintuitive" when they are nothing of the kind. What the speakers mean in these instances is that the conclusions *seem irrational* because they run counter to the comfortable (il)logic of our prejudices and assumptions, or arise from processes of logic with which we are quite unfamiliar. The word "counterintuitive" has in these cases been ripped loose from its moorings and set adrift in the muddied sea of feelings — not true perceptions — from whence it is casually and conveniently plucked to describe something that only *feels* strange and only *seems* unreasonable.

In fact, where real science is involved, the conclusions reached are (like Juan Burdeniuc's) wholly logical, and very likely may have been furthered by moments of genuine intuition on the part of the scientists who came up with them. Being new, such conclusions challenge our comfortable, established ways of thinking. Trying to get comfortable again by misappropriating language meant to describe a legitimate, nonlinear grasp of trends and events is not a particularly good idea.

Intuition yields extraordinary results in activities where inventiveness is critical to success. Looked at from a certain vantage point, intuition is also the faculty that allows us to navigate time as we navigate physical space with our "ordinary" senses: it attempts to tell us *when* a given course of action is wise or foolish. Its recommendations are often neither blanket approvals nor blanket condemnations of a class of behavior; rather, instead of an unqualified yes, intuition says, "Yes — *right away*," and instead of an unqualified no, it often says, "Not *now*."

If you remain skeptical, I offer this anecdote, somewhat more dramatic than mine about the Occidental-Niagara incident.

There is an international activist (I'll call her Elaine) who works on environmental issues in a part of the world where life is often dangerous because of ongoing conflicts between the government and various opposing factions. On one of her return visits to the United States she told me of traveling through one of the riskier parts of the region in which she works. She was riding in a truck driven by a colleague when they were flagged down by a soldier at the roadside.

"You might not want to go further on this road today," said the soldier. "There were some mines down there this morning. We did sweep the area, but it might be better to wait until tomorrow, when we have time to check it more thoroughly."

The driver of the vehicle, hearing that a mine-clearing operation had been performed, was happy to convince himself that there was no real threat in continuing on that road. Doubtless it would have been a significant inconvenience to wait until morning or to travel by a different route. In his mind — or more particularly, in the left half of it — the sense of looming inconvenience outweighed the probability of danger. He elected to press on.

Elaine told me that from approximately the moment the soldier spoke, she knew with absolute certainty that the road was mined. This had nothing to do with trust or mistrust of the soldier, or even with reasonable assumptions about the marginal reliability of minesweeping operations. She simply *knew* that it would not do to go further on that road. She told me how she tried to convince the driver that a little circumspection in this case could do no harm. Her efforts were fruitless. In the end, true to her own wisdom and unwilling — even perhaps blessedly unable — to ignore its dictates, she insisted on climbing out of the truck and finding another way to get where she was going. The driver, deaf to her urgings, went on. Some distance down the road he hit a mine, one either missed by the sweepers or replanted by guerilla forces after the government troops had left the area. The truck was destroyed and the driver was killed.

* * *

The importance of developing and acknowledging intuition goes beyond sensing the likely outcome of a particular action on one particular day: it goes to the matter of choosing whole areas of investigation, commitment, and application. That the line between microcosmic and global choices is somewhat artificial becomes apparent, of course, when a single action is found to demonstrably (linearly) affect an entire enterprise.

A hard lesson of this kind was experienced (though not quite learned, I think) at Greenpeace in 1995, during the ultimately successful effort to prevent Royal Dutch Shell from sinking the disused Brent Spar oil platform in the North Atlantic. The group's campaigners twice occupied the rig, garnering extraordinary publicity, as it was being towed out to sea. This otherwise highly effective campaign nearly fell apart when an unnecessary, incompletely researched choice was made to take sludge samples from vent pipes rather than from the platform's storage tanks themselves. This decision led to a hugely inaccurate estimate of the amount of polluting material still contained in the Brent Spar. The case against dumping such a rig at sea had already been made and was reasonable from the outset — even based on Shell's own admitted figures — and the unit did, in fact, contain up to 100 metric tons of residues, as later independently confirmed by a team of investigators in Norway. But Greenpeace took a tremendous hit in some sectors of the media for bringing forward an estimate of over fifty times that amount. We thereafter issued a public apology for the error (though by no means for the campaign) and in apologizing distinguished ourselves from our corporate adversaries, but the incident was a costly one.

I have no doubt that the action taken aboard Brent Spar appeared reasonable to those involved at the time. What events proved was not just that they lacked sufficient factual knowledge (in this case of the rig's structure and its implications), but that in the absence of this knowledge they had no *functional* resource to fall back on. A consciously and deliberately intuitive individual in their place would at the critical moment have looked to a different area of perception. A generalized awareness of the soundness of the sampling procedure would in all likelihood have been available to such a person. One either understands that such intuition is real and can be cultivated, or denies it and goes on half-blind into the night. It would be helpful both to Greenpeace and to the culture if the group should choose to be in the forefront of the cultivation. It is a great irony that many Greenpeace staff of my acquaintance have been highly intuitive individuals but unconsciously so, and they have therefore made numerous choices out of their right hemispheres without ever fully acknowledging the fact.

Let me here acknowledge that learning to recognize real intuition and isolate it from other perceptions, emotions, and sensations can be greatly challenging. (It took a fairly rigorous course of training to introduce me fully to my own intuition. I had previously misidentified it countless times.) On the other hand, I find I have limited patience for people who dismiss as "just coincidence" such a confluence of perception and event as Elaine experienced. And I'm afraid I give very short shrift to people who dismiss such confluence as being universally the subsequent fantasy or fabrication of the perceiver.

Intuition exists. We may quite legitimately ask whether it is operative at a given moment, but it is intellectually dishonest to dismiss it entirely in the face of a rather massive body of collected evidence. It is a very poor idea to ignore its existence and pass by opportunities to learn how to recognize and enhance it.

I am equally opposed to romanticizing the faculty and to cheapening such a skill by sensationalizing it. And I am particularly unhappy with those who insist that they are conversant with intuition when they are not. Lying to oneself or to the general public about the possession of such a skill can deepen the skepticism of others who desperately need to acknowledge their own intuitive skills, and it can place obstacles in the path of those seeking ways to develop an ability they dimly or partially sense but cannot yet clearly identify.

For individuals, attending to one's intuition may be a matter of life and death. And the same may be true for the body collective of humanity on this planet. It is difficult to get the benefit of such a faculty when one's culture labors systematically to deny its existence — the more so when the culture is so far into sleep that it rarely even acknowledges that denial is taking place. Yes, the exercise of intuition stretches us well beyond our usual, comfortable boundaries, but it is a great blessing to have this faculty among our native abilities nonetheless. There is great reassurance in learning that we did not come here without the equipment necessary to navigate the whole of our reality.

Most readers of this book have been born into a culture that has tried to boil reality down to a minimum, and unfortunately has gone near to cooking itself in its own pot. But the premise of this book is that the individual who deeply chooses to create is not held hostage to the workings of a given culture, society, or political system. Nor is such an individual finally subject to the will of any other person. Whatever obstacles may be presented by these external influences, each of us may shake the frame of

Earth as powerfully and effectively as any other, *given sufficient mobilization of spirit*. Neither intuition nor intellect is alone the tool sufficient to all aims and situations, and indeed there may be some resource above both.

In this culture, however, where one form or another of the workings of intellect has so long effectively occupied the position of the Golden Calf, a rather essential starting point for the would-be artist/activist is the simple acknowledgment that associative, nonlinear connections between events, trends, and people *are* often perceptible.

Chapter Nine

An Echo at Alcatraz

M_y friend Red Elk was trained as a medicine man of the Blackfoot, and although by his own admission he is long out of practice, his training still affects many aspects of his life and being. His routines are fairly ordinary, but the unusual has some tendency to seek him out — not, I think, entirely by accident.

Like other Native Americans I know, having been raised in traditions such as the vision quest and the sense that Spirit readily communicates to the willing listener, Red Elk regards matter-of-factly both the idea of intuition as a functional resource and the concept that vision (and creative visualization, though he may not formally practice it) has great power.[1] From early on in our friendship I have also sensed in him and in his wife, Sweet Image, whose heritage is Crow, a quality of peacefulness that transcended the sometimes eventful daily circumstances of their lives. It is reminiscent of something I have sensed in certain Buddhist monks I have met.

At one point after my own path had led me to Greenpeace, I had a telephone conversation with Red Elk in which he told me that he had recently paid a visit to the local property of a large waste-hauling firm and documented on videotape certain illegal practices of the company. Anyone familiar with large corporations of this type will appreciate that bearing witness to their activities in this way is a serious business involving certain notable risks, and is not to be entered into lightly. The situation subsequently intensified when he informed the company that he had recorded their transgressions. There followed some provocative exchanges — first with them and next with the authorities, who became profoundly and aggressively interested in the videotape. Ultimately and somewhat unexpectedly, federal legal action was taken against the firm, a bracing experience costing it about two million dollars in fines.

I found several aspects of this event striking. First was the simple *rightness* of the thing — a Native American, with a shaman's authority, squaring off against a corporation that neatly symbolized everything that is unworkable about the society which usurped the lands, the rights, and the material opportunities of the first peoples of this continent. Although an isolated act, it was one resulting in unique and quite poetic justice, and it struck me as satisfying (and deeply amusing, at the company's expense) right down to the level of the soul.

Second, I found myself aware that the same action taken by one less centered than Red Elk could have been sheer bravado; but for him, though it was a new avenue of expression, it struck me as remarkably natural. I did not expect him to make a habit of such enterprises, but as I pictured him carrying off this particular event at this particular stage of his existence, I thought that it was almost predictable and to him not necessarily any more dramatic than going out for groceries or picking up a package at the post office.[2] For a given person at a certain time, the extraordinary can be very normal.

Third, I did not think it coincidental that such an action was carried out by someone with Red Elk's background: he had brought much of the essence of his training and of Blackfoot spiritual traditions with him into his life far from any historical territory of the Blackfoot people, and integrated it into the routines of his daily existence.

Finally, I did not think it coincidental that Red Elk involved himself in an environmental issue at about the same time I was becoming immersed in the activities and philosophies of Greenpeace. The threads of human interconnection are often invisible. We affect one another more than we know, and we especially affect those to whom we are close — not necessarily physically nor even emotionally close, but nearby, if you like, in spirit. Many of the mechanisms by which this happens (everything from simple conversation to competitive impulses) are linear and more or less visible; others are invisible and mysteriously associative, and not so easily perceived or identified. Thoreau suggested something in this vein when he wrote, "What wealth it is to have such friends that we cannot think of them without a sense of elevation."

Red Elk's activities at the waste-hauler's facility suggest an individual paradigm for activism that is deeply founded in the human spirit and influenced by traditions of the spirit. Whatever mutual reinforcement existed between him and myself suggests another. The paradigms are small, but like many such paradigms, might be seen to have larger implications: the significant, spiritual force of nonviolent, risk-based witness by Native Americans; the latent power of corrective, and creative, interactions between Native Americans and the American culture which today, its conscience fitfully dozing, surrounds them. That collective conscience has not often been perceptibly aroused on behalf of the first peoples, but modern history does provide a record of some exceptions.

*   *   *

The Sean Connery–Nicholas Cage thriller *The Rock*, which takes the phrase "action film" to exhaustive extremes, is set amid the grim relic that was Alcatraz Prison. The film is no great cultural coup. But it does get across an interesting physical sense of what it is like to be on the Rock. Like the film itself, the setting is not notably conducive to spiritual pursuits or to a reflective frame of mind.

A little less outwardly dramatic than the movie and almost forgotten by the general public is an event that took place on Alcatraz almost thirty years ago. I think about it from time to time because of my relationships with American Indian activist colleagues and friends, some of whom were there. I am referring to the island's eighteen-month occupation, initially by a group of fourteen Native Americans and subsequently by the larger community of the "Hundred Warriors," with the attendant demand that the Rock be permanently returned to Indian control. This event took place a few years after the prison had been abandoned by the federal government.

The seizure of Alcatraz was designed as a symbolic action rather than an armed confrontation. (The Hundred Warriors had among them not much beyond a few bows and arrows, whose menace was pretty much ceremonial.) It was in its first phase relatively organized and highly visible, and something of a success where public relations was concerned. The occupiers bore witness to the centuries-long attack on their peoples and their cultural fabric with intensity, yet with a degree of gracefulness and, as a sort of secret weapon of last resort, a sense of grim humor and irony. This last was displayed in a brilliantly conceived manifesto that went beyond the Indians' legal claim to

Alcatraz Island (one of many properties to which, under a treaty of 1868, certain tribes had claim once active federal use had ceased). Deadpan, it proclaimed the singular qualities of the place that logically made it — by established government standards — entirely appropriate for transfer to the tribes. The island was, it noted, stony, barren, isolated, largely unsuitable for human habitation and sustenance, and (having been wholly made over into a prison) perfectly designed to separate its occupants from the society at large while holding their welfare hostage to the whims of that society. In short, Alcatraz Island was much like the land allotted by the government for the average Indian reservation.

The activities of the Hundred Warriors, and of supporters moving back and forth between the prison and the mainland, involved substantial risks. At the outset they could not feel sure of the public response to their actions, nor (more immediately) of the response of governmental authority, particularly law enforcement agencies. As it turned out, a Coast Guard blockade of the island was imposed, and — more ominously — a fairly massive armed assault was initially planned under the auspices of the General Services Administration; it was put off by the action of one decent-minded official and finally cancelled when the White House became directly involved in the situation.[3] Possibly the greatest risk, however, was that over time the Indians would be psychologically overwhelmed by the sheer, stark tedium of Alcatraz, and debilitated in soul by the wasteland the European American penal system had made of the little island.

The initial mindset of the occupiers and their means of organizing themselves were influenced by everything from experience in Vietnam (a number were veterans) to the tenor of the times (which tended toward the politically and behaviorally liberal). Asserting a strong legal and moral claim through nonviolent occupation dovetailed with antiwar activities then taking place throughout the culture; promoting the cause through relatively sophisticated public relations gave the issue a rare profile. The action also emerged from a background of distinct and deeply honorable tribal spiritual traditions, which it brought forward into a new time in a form well suited to that time — and in a way that made its message accessible to millions of people who might otherwise have passed it by. It was a modern variation on counting coup, the Indian tradition of riding into the midst of one's enemies and making physical contact, not to do physical harm but to demonstrate courage, spiritual power, and great skill.

At ground level the Alcatraz occupation was a gritty affair, well matched to the surroundings. The harsh physical conditions in the run-down old prison took their toll (though some Indians had experienced conditions almost as bad on their reservations); tribal backgrounds were various, and personalities and agendas became increasingly discordant; alcohol was a predictable problem; a fair quantity of drugs were consumed well outside the auspices of traditional ceremonial usage. Its outward raggedness notwithstanding, the event — simultaneously earthy and principled — contained an echo of greatness past.

I would go further and say that it embodied a quality of greatness in the modern day. Though a deep and just anger fueled the event, the action finally assaulted only the fatuous pride of too many non–Native Americans in a false history of our country. Set in the context of a prevailing Native American psychology which, as some professional clinicians have pointed out, is (logically enough) similar to that of Holocaust survivors, it appears all the more remarkable. In retrospect it seems a rather shining moment, one that united the members of many tribes, with many traditions and languages, as little has done in the modern era. However disillusioning the decline of organization and morale over the year and a half of occupation (a respectable period to maintain an esprit de corps given the nature of the real estate), strategically and even spiritually it was a brilliantly conceived event.

In a sense it was also the high-water mark to date — in terms of its impact on the popular mind and the popular political will — of the movement for justice for Native Americans. Four years later at Wounded Knee, South Dakota, the lengthy armed confrontation between federal forces and members of the American Indian Movement — who claimed the site where Big Foot and his people had been massacred in 1890 — would erode public enthusiasm and support for the Native American cause. Arguably, the coup de grace come in 1975 with the shooting of two FBI agents at nearby Pine Ridge and the subsequent controversial conviction of AIM member Leonard Peltier. Armed resistance momentarily raised the Indian spirit, but violence as a long-term strategy did not work greatly in favor of AIM. Neither did it enhance the reputation of the FBI, which cast itself in the role of villain even in the minds of many who condemned the shooting of its agents.[4] But the negative public response focused primarily on Native Americans, whose minimal interface with the culture at large suffered as a consequence. Territorial and economic gains since made in the courts, and the casinos, cannot entirely offset the lack of a deeper public enlightenment.

There was another tragedy in these events that is seldom remarked: Americans who elected to make Wounded Knee an excuse for hardening their hearts toward Indian peoples foreclosed for themselves the option of helping to right the injustices of five post-Columbian centuries. That foreclosure by themselves on their own spirits is a loss not to be minimized — *all the more so* in a culture that routinely insists on minimizing it. A great many people thus made themselves, in a sense, unconscious victims of the event.

Still, some residual legacies of an enthusiasm generated at the time of the Alcatraz occupation remain — both evidenced and nurtured by such phenomena as the success of the Oscar-winning film *Dances With Wolves.* Jog the memory of a thoughtful non–Native American old enough to recall the taking of the Rock, and ask what she or he thought of it at the time: likely as not you will get a smile and an acknowledgment that, as in Red Elk's confrontation with the waste-haulers, there was something poetically just about the residency of the Hundred Warriors. I suspect that even in these allegedly conservative times, a majority of Americans would just as soon the federal government had not driven the occupiers from the island (in June of 1971), but simply handed over title to the place and let the Indians make a cultural center of it, as they had intended. Had it done so early on, incidentally, a subsequent history is conceivable in which the 1973 Wounded Knee confrontation would never have taken place. Swiftly allowing the Hundred Warriors the small victory — and the legal justice — of keeping Alcatraz might have forestalled some of the desperation that fueled later AIM activities and generated the violent standoff with the federals.

While I was drafting this chapter, my attention was synchronously drawn to the following quote from a *Christian Science Monitor* article:

> The great dream of most of the 2 million Indians in the United States is to walk in both worlds, to participate in mainstream society and yet preserve their traditional tribal cultures.[5]

In a sense different from that imagined by the author of this quotation, Alcatraz was a walk in both worlds. It was tribal culture physically overlaying itself on one abandoned corner of mainstream society, and symbolically insisting that society *pay attention* and *make room*. It was an ethical, assertive move toward the establishment of an order in which justice for the first peoples would be an actual phenomenon, not a theoretical concept. No great thing is ever precisely duplicated, but many more right actions — and even some occupations — might constructively arise from the paradigm of the taking of the Rock.

It is telling that the piece of (alleged) Native American oratory most quoted outside the boundaries of Indian reservations is an improperly attributed piece from the hand of a screenwriter, the famous so-called Chief Seattle speech.[6] The speech entire is a moving work, and writer Ted Perry, who shaped it in the early 1970s, did in fact take some passages from a translation of remarks made in the mid-1850s by Seattle, the chief of the Duwamish. (The translation was, of course, done by a European American, a Dr. Henry Smith.) Perry may well deserve some kind of an Oscar for his version of the thing. But while I love much of his speech, its existence and its regular (ab)use are symptomatic of the gap between popular views of Native American culture and history, and an actual accounting of them.

To cite just one jarring example, as pointed out in an article in the journal *Environmental Ethics*,[7] even the (arguable) translation of Seattle's actual remarks indicates that he did *not* say, as Perry's character does,

> One thing we know . . . our God is the same God . . . and his compassion is equal for the red man and the white.

but rather,

> Your God is not our God! Your God loves your people and hates mine. . . . He has forsaken His red children. . . . The white man's God cannot love our people or He would protect them.

The Perry text, written for a film produced by the Southern Baptist Convention, has beauty and truth enough in its own right, but the old translation goes a great deal nearer the Indian experience of the onslaught of an alien culture largely bent on exterminating the native inhabitants of this continent.

It is hard to accurately assess today's progress when you have lost touch with yesterday. This is doubly true if you are looking at the past through a rosy mist of pseudospiritual wishful thinking, as many do who quote Perry in ignorance of the real Chief Seattle and the circumstances of his time. The difficulty with Perry's script lies in the confusion between its wonderful articulation of a number of elevated truths and the existence of some far less pleasant and uplifting historical ones. It is important to grasp *both* to appreciate what has been wrought thus far in the relation between Native Americans and modern American culture, how much remains to be accomplished, and what the culture at large could gain from a genuine interaction with the first peoples.

All of us stand to benefit from tribal traditions of deliberate, right-spirited appreciation of what flows from the Creator. Native American culture also models for the rest of us a receptivity to wisdom and the urgings of spirit. In theory, Christianity also embraces these principles; in practice, with the rarest of exceptions, it falls terribly short. I am a Christian myself, with a deep attachment to the core of my religion. At the same time, some of the most powerfully religious moments I have experienced have been in Indian sweat lodges, where I have had to contend with my own arrogance and explore the meaning of humility. I am speaking of experiences beyond intellect and extending also beyond the boundaries of emotion. The moments have been distinct, and additive — not replicative of religious experiences I have had in church or elsewhere.

I am not exalting Native American practices above my own tradition or any other, but I am testifying: there is something to be gained by crossing the divide. I am keenly aware that the sharing of Indian traditions and practices is the subject of sharp debate within the Native American community, and has been subject to abuse by non-Indians. But I have to trust that Native Americans will forgive me for holding to a vision of a future in which those who will truly gain from such experiences will be allowed to undergo them.

In speaking to Native American friends about courses in creativity that I have studied and taught — which do not borrow specifically from Indian tradition — I have occasionally, and only mildly tongue-in-cheek, described such programs as "vision quest for Anglos." The vision quest is, in one form, the ancient, rigorous practice of the young warrior going alone, apart from the tribe, and attaining a sacred state of meditative or higher consciousness in which he receives a transformative picture that directs his life as Spirit intends it.[8] The Native American spiritual tradition holds a deep understanding of the character and the consequences of such true individual vision and a commitment to it. "Vision" is no buzzword in Indian culture. It refers to something which owns a reality in several of the astrophysicist's or mathematician's alternative dimensions, and which when deeply pursued affects the three familiar ones beyond most non-Indians' usual imaginings. European American culture, on the other hand, has never really had any accepted rite of passage that challenges individuals (or societies) to deliberately seek a high and worthy vision, much less make an actual commitment to manifesting one in this world. But think again of the hologram: society is transformed through the transformation of its individual members.

Those who accept the workings of such a vision in their lives are willing to tolerate discomfort in the service of its manifestation. The willingness to tolerate such stress arises from committing utterly to an ideal while standing amidst the checkered landscape of an imperfect present. Pretty much by definition, it cannot be a comfortable situation. Genuine activism involves idealism, and a dedication to an ideal has always placed the individual at odds with the mass of humanity, who may like the idea of sharing an ideal but regularly resist the implications of doing so.

The individual who truly loves this world (and all its citizens) comes, sooner or later, to realize that what passes for realism with most people is nothing of the kind, and, simultaneously, that what is labelled idealism comes nearer to the laws of true reality than the so-called realism does. You cannot be a "realist" when you are in essential revolt — conscious or not — against the most fundamental principles on which reality stands. And the large truth is that reality shifts in our favor — has always shifted and presumably always will shift — as a consequence of the dedicated thought and action of people who attach themselves irremovably to an ideal and back up their stand by living in large accordance with it. Most people have tended to accept the idea that "things can't be changed" because it is more comfortable to think that way than to do the work necessary to transform the world. Fortunately for all of us, there have always been people who see through the smokescreen.

True realism is idealism with teeth. It implies a clear and worthy vision of the desirable future, an acknowledgment of how far we have come and how great a distance yet remains to be traveled, and the willingness to go that distance, whether the trip is comfortable or not.

The quest of the broad American culture for comfort and security has nearly supplanted its quest for visions.[9] But in the face of genocide, uprooting from their rightful territories, and every imaginable cultural and individual insult, the shamans and other wise souls among the first peoples have kept alive the flame of the old traditions. And the tribes, collectively, have never therefore quite forgotten the wonderful, terrible truth that one's high humanity depends on the ability to be the walking *locus in terra* of a worthwhile dream, and to embody it at any cost. In the midst of a contemporary American spiritual landscape that sometimes seems to resemble the terrain of Alcatraz, this wisdom remains available to those who are spirited enough to seek it out.

Chapter Ten

The Message
from Dharamsala

In the late winter of 1993, a few months after my wife and I moved to southern California from New England, the Los Angeles Greenpeace office passed along to me an invitation from the local Tibetan community. It was requested that a Greenpeace speaker attend a commemorative gathering in the city. The occasion was the annual March 10 remembrance of the 1959 uprising against the Chinese forces occupying Tibet, an uprising that cost the lives of tens of thousands of Tibetans and resulted in the Dalai Lama's journey into exile in northern India, at Dharamsala. The commemoration to which Greenpeace was invited was to be held at the doors of the Chinese consulate.

I had had a minor education in the modern history of Tibet, and it had made a lasting impression.[1] I knew that Chinese communist forces had invaded Tibet in 1949–50 and initiated a process of cultural genocide that continues to this day. In addition to waves of killings over the five decades, the religious tradition of Tibetan Buddhism was placed under unrelieved siege; some six thousand temples were destroyed, and it is now illegal for Tibetan citizens even to display pictures of the Dalai Lama in their own homes. So many ethnic Chinese have been imported into the country that they outnumber Tibetans. The countryside has been ravaged, and when the great photographer Galen Rowell visited Tibet during the 1980s, only in its most remote regions could he find the country's wildlife in its natural abundance.

In a comparatively recent development, the Chinese kidnapped the six-year-old boy declared by Buddhists to be the latest reincarnation of the Panchen Lama (the second most revered figure in their religion, after the Dalai Lama himself); they simultaneously incarcerated the senior monk who was the boy's nearest protector. They next selected their own candidate to replace the boy, put forward another monk as his guardian, and gave vague or false reports to the world of the welfare and whereabouts of the true Panchen Lama and his protector. These actions were met in the world community with a collective indifference like that which once (despite the vocal efforts of some) greeted Kristallnacht. I draw that parallel quite deliberately: the widespread ignorance of the Tibetan situation has a fairly exact parallel in the refusal of many people to accept or act on reports of the atrocities being perpetrated against the Jews during the Second World War. Americans remain preoccupied with Taiwan, which has had fifty years of freedom and is armed to the teeth, but Tibet, enslaved (in territory, not spirit) for nearly as long as Taiwan has been autonomous, yet awaits a response fractionally as dramatic.

At the time I received the invitation to the Tibetan demonstration in Los Angeles, I was aware of many of the above facts. I was also aware of the deep connection between the Dalai Lama's philosophy and practice of nonviolence and the Quaker principle of peaceful witness on which Greenpeace was founded. I had met two of the Chinese students, Li Lu and Pei Minxin, who played significant parts in organizing and publicizing, respectively, the student-led Chinese pro-democracy movement that culminated in the confrontation at Tiananmen Square. For these and many other reasons, I was intensely interested in supporting all efforts of the Tibetans in this country to make their cause better known and understood, and I was quite interested in at least symbolically confronting the Chinese government.

I arrived at the Chinese consulate well past sunset. A score or so of hand-held candles flickered at the edge of its tiny, darkened lawn and lit the faces of the modest gathering of Tibetans and their supporters. Several Buddhist monks, in their robes, stood among the group. A small public address system was being set up at the edge of the sidewalk, and two or three of the demonstration's organizers were huddled over it. The consulate itself seemed dark and cold, and I wondered what its occupants thought about the little temporary community on their doorstep. I was sure they were quite aware of our presence, and almost equally sure that they would make no acknowledgment of it.

I think it may be a little difficult for most Westerners to imagine what it is like to stand among Tibetan exiles before an outpost of the Chinese government. One might begin by imagining what it would have been like to stand before a German consulate during the days of the Third Reich with twenty or thirty people of the Jewish faith. With the Tibetans, however, there is the added element of the conscious Tibetan Buddhist commitment to nonviolence, which affects everything about such an event. A candlelight vigil among these people is not only a commemoration of a past event, nor is it only a lamentation of loss. It takes place in the context of an overarching vision of what is possible for a sane humanity. For every moment of sadness there exists a parallel universe of recognition. The world we dream of hovers just a little above our heads. A Tibetan commemoration is, finally, more invitation than lament: it is the making of a place (perhaps only momentarily; perhaps somewhat more than that) into which the desired future may be born. It is a place that exists consistent with the rules of existence of the future, manifested *now.*

In her book *Culture and Commitment*, the great anthropologist Margaret Mead noted that where Westerners see the past as fixed and immutable, some Polynesian cultures see it as fluid, and that where we see the future as primarily fluid, the Polynesians tend to see it as preexisting at a certain point but awaiting birth, like the child in the womb. Their concentration thus rests on making wise preparation for the birth of the new reality. A similar orientation, with a more conscious, focused spirituality, appears to exist among Tibetan Buddhists. It is an orientation of much faith, without the rhetoric of faith that often accompanies Christian adventures in the area.

This orientation involves a great and personal investment in the coming world, and at the same time, in keeping with the Dalai Lama's philosophy of compassion, it retains a great awareness of the difficulties faced in the world of the present by one's adversaries as well as by one's colleagues and oneself. There is no room in it for hatred, nor even for cynicism. It requires, gently but firmly, one's great attentiveness to the prospect of *wellness for all* in a very deep sense. It is thus an extraordinary paradigm for the orientation of creative activism, and particularly for the mental and emotional orientation of activists taking part in specific events.

In earlier chapters I spoke of the power of visualization — and more particularly of a fully perceived *vision* of an individual or collective future — to mobilize the resources of human creative consciousness and ultimately to yield remarkable transformations in the world at hand. I mentioned the impact of a deeply experienced spirituality, and the highly effective positive images it lodges in the subconscious, on the lifepaths of certain people. I also suggested that through its imagery this deep spirituality yields a core resilience and a willingness to tolerate short-term discouragement and defeat in the pursuit of long-term goals. The vision of a peaceful and compassionate world held by the Dalai Lama and those who follow his teachings is surely among the most powerful and the most beautiful of such image systems. It is held by Tibetan Buddhists, and many Tibetans who are not practicing Buddhists, in a very large sense on behalf of all the rest of us, quite as much as it is held for the benefit of Tibet. For the last fifty years the path of the Tibetan people has been a steep one. But they have walked it to the great and lasting benefit of many besides themselves, including many who are largely ignorant of the Tibetan situation.

As one among a number of speakers that night on that Los Angeles sidewalk before the Chinese consulate, I did not talk very long. But I doubt that any remarks of mine have ever come more from the heart. I tried to express the debt owed, in one sense, by all of us who are at the work of improving the world, to the Tibetan people. What they have chosen, under the gentle, powerful influence of the Dalai Lama, is to embody a higher way of living. They are drawing us all forward. Progress may seem so slow as to be imperceptible — and there remains the question of whether the rest of us will choose to do our part and pick up the pace — but in some way we are all affected. It is an influence as subtle and yet as utterly suasive as the solar wind.

In the late summer of 1995, a half-dozen veteran Greenpeace activists from several countries flew to Beijing, gathered in Tiananmen Square, and staged what was quite possibly the briefest protest in the organization's history. It was also one of the most daring and significant.

In keeping with its vigorous protests of the renewed French nuclear tests in the Pacific, the organization concluded that as a matter of consistency at the least it was essential to address the continuing Chinese tests as well. It was further concluded that witness should be borne in this case in as direct and powerful a manner as possible. Thus it was that the six activists planned to pay a visit to the site of the 1989 confrontation between China's aging, militaristic leadership and the student movement of its young, oncoming, idealistic generation. The choice of location was both symbolic and practical. It was a tribute to those who took part in the country's pro-democracy movement, and it drew the focus of the international media.

On entering the square, the six unfurled and held up a long narrow banner which said, in English and Chinese, "Stop All Nuclear Testing!" In less than a minute, Chinese plainclothes police rushed forward and tore the banner from their hands. The six were taken into custody, interrogated for some thirty hours (the authorities were incredulous that they could have carried off the protest without any assistance from Chinese citizens), and promptly deported. Thus one of the brighter moments in Greenpeace history swiftly came and went.

The direct connection between this demonstration and the situation in Tibet is that the Chinese government has placed nuclear missiles, a nuclear waste dump, and a nuclear test site at various locations in the Tibetan countryside. These actions were not taken in a cultural vacuum. The Chinese leadership well knows exactly what the Dalai Lama stands for, and the placement of these facilities is a deliberate insult and a renewed assault on the Tibetan people, calculated to heighten a sense of powerlessness among the citizenry. Perhaps it will have the intended emotional impact, perhaps not. I doubt very much, however, that it will ultimately erode the spiritual strength of the Tibetan people.

Fifty years of communism have done little to improve the Chinese leadership's grasp of basic principles of spirituality, or of creativity. This is hardly surprising, given the nature of the beast they are riding — or rather, *think* they are riding, for in truth they are well inside the belly of the thing and have no consciousness of the fact. They have likewise not the least consciousness of the strength and durability of those gentle forces to which they have set themselves in opposition both in Tibet and within China itself. As was well said by one of China's greatest souls, Lao-tzu, water is "of all things most yielding," but in time turns rock to silt and carries it away. Contemporary China's day is passing, perhaps more quickly than most imagine, and only the greatest and most intensely focused creative effort will enable it to yet bring forth that new dawn which should have come at Tiananmen Square. China's leaders would weep bitterly if they knew what they had lost by standing in defiance of the will of the coming generations for freedom, which also was a greater Will. I speak of what they have lost for *themselves*. Those

Christian perceptions in which I was raised see the unrepentant oppressor as suffering at last far the greater (self-inflicted) injury in such a case. I do not take such perceptions, nor were they ever intended, as figures of speech.

That apparently infinite store of goodwill from which the Dalai Lama brings forth his personal vision of Tibet, which he sees as becoming a "Zone of Peace," extends also to the people and even to the leaders of China. (This is so even though by accepted estimates the Chinese occupation has cost the lives of over a million Tibetans — more than a sixth of the population.) As a Christian I marvel at the magnitude of this extension of Grace and forgiveness. It is the conclusive demonstration to me, if I needed one, of the seeming paradox of distinct yet coexistent and even mutually supportive theologies. Buddhism is not Christianity, nor are the two likely to blur into one another in the visible future. Yet here the world finds the (arguably) greatest lesson of Christianity embodied for any to see who have eyes to observe it — and for any to experience who have a heart they will open to it — by a Buddhist monk and his followers.

The Dalai Lama's "Five Point Peace Plan for Tibet," set forth at the Congressional Human Rights Caucus in Washington in 1987 and reiterated in an address to the European Parliament at Strasbourg in 1988, contains the following proposals:

1) All of traditional Tibet should become a zone of "Ahimsa" (the Hindi term for a state of peace and nonviolence).

2) China must end its "population transfer" policy, by which the Tibetans have become a minority in their own country.

3) Human rights and democracy must be restored in Tibet, and the people must be free to exercise their spirituality and the full measure of their own cultural, social, and economic practices.

4) The Tibetan natural environment must be restored, and the presence of nuclear weapons and nuclear waste in Tibet must come to an end.

5) Genuine negotiations on Tibet's future, and the future relationship between Tibet and China, must be initiated.

It is a vision which, brought to fruition, would immeasurably benefit China itself along with Tibet. It would create a buffer zone between China and India which would minimize the tensions between those countries; it would preserve the Tibetan natural resource base, which unchecked Chinese rapaciousness is now rapidly undermining, for the potential benefit of both Tibetans *and* Chinese; and it would bring to China a degree of international acceptance and approval, which the country has sought so intensely in recent years (most notably in its failed bid for the Olympic Games of the year 2000) but has shown itself dramatically undeserving of by its wretched and impoverished refusal to acknowledge accepted international standards of human rights.

If there is something particular for Western culture to learn from the focus on the powerful vision of an individual in Native American traditions, there is also something particular for us to learn from Tibetan Buddhism about a collective vision and its importance to the future of us all. Tibetan activism is a model of long-term investment in the well-being of the earth and of the human species. The Tibetan national vision, as articulated and embodied by the Dalai Lama, is in a sense subservient to a larger vision of the earth. This larger vision, insofar as I can grasp it, is wholly consistent with the vision of the new Eden, of a peaceful world attained through peaceful means and of an interrelationship between humans and nature that is perpetual. The core vision of other spiritual and religious groups such as the Quakers may be equivalent, but such groups do not anywhere exist as nation-states. The case of Tibet is unique.

The Tibetan situation therefore exists as a kind of litmus test of other nations' commitment to the future, and of the commitment of individuals as well. The uniqueness of the Tibetan people, their culture, and their circumstances suggests strongly to me that they are a singular and literal gift to the world and that their situation holds a singular lesson for us. This gift is accompanied by a rare attendant responsibility. We are offered the chance to support a culture which is of the (visionary) future, adhering to laws elsewhere ignored or trampled even while existing *in* the present world. The situation is ultimately a kind of litmus test not just for the moral and creative health of nations, but for the success of the human experiment. It is a doorway into the possible future of a world that is deserving of such goodness, even greatness, as the Tibetans embody.

Chapter Eleven

The Media and the Mythos

Next to a preoccupation with direct fundraising, no broad, materially based, strategic concern so preoccupies contemporary activists as does getting the attention of the media. It is perhaps an inevitable corollary that aside from a conventional approach to fundraising, few greater specific impediments to the human creative spirit exist in our work than the assumption that the media must be dealt with on its own conventional terms — and formulaically.

I have already indicated that Greenpeace's first great media coup — international coverage of its initial confrontation with the Soviet whaling fleet in 1975 — occurred as much through indirect, associative, and rationally unpredictable processes as through linear, well-reasoned, and conventional ones. It is not my intention to demean the thoughtful, vigorous, and well-timed use of the latter. Obviously, though, it is very much my intention to make the case that rational means exist in a context considerably larger than the demonstrably rational.

In the end, whether we are Buddhists, Muslims, Hindus, Taoists, Shintoists, Jews, Christians, Confucianists, or practitioners of any other genuinely spiritual tradition, we must make a basic decision. We must either accept the wisdom, evoked in one form or another by every true religion, that there is more going on here than can be defined by the material alone — or comprehended fully by the rational mind — or we must risk spiritual impoverishment and debilitation. And in the end there really is something for the creative soul to gain from that part of traditional religious wisdom contained in the idea of faith. I am referring particularly to faith in the possibility of benevolent results manifesting by nonlinear and unpredictable means, which as a purely *structural* matter allows for the invitation of creative, associative processes into one's life. The "something" to be gained can only be accessed through the practice of the principles of creativity, however feeble and inconsistent our initial efforts may appear. Its benefits cannot be obtained through debate about the validity of these principles, rational discourse on their nature and essence, or a wistful supposition that their rewards must be reserved for the spiritually advanced.

All this comes down to cases in a hurry when activists are confronted with the business of bringing the world's attention to bear on major issues of the day via the media.

Few circumstances more easily elicit a tendency to manipulation than does a need for attention. This principle is evidenced in human affairs from the infancy of the individual through the adolescence of nations. A whole range of superficial reactive-responsive mechanisms in human consciousness may be brought instantly to bear when we require the support and assistance of others. The infant cries when it wants food, then discovers the broader efficacy of the technique for getting its parents' attention, and it is a rare parent who can intuitively discern when the infant's need is genuine and when it is not. In adulthood we individually and collectively retain the long-rooted assumption that the loudest cry — or, more cleverly, the most unique or the most engaging — will elicit the most immediate and satisfactory response from a particular caregiver. This central assumption is evident in any number of the press releases, public activities, and private discussions of many organizations nominally dedicated to shaping a new and better world. (As I have said before, it is one thing to inherently possess an attractive or impressive style; it is another thing to abuse style as a manipulative device.)

I leave it to you to judge the maturity of this (largely unconscious) dynamic in human affairs, and to decide whether this is the sort of dynamic you would wish to see carried forward into our individual and collective life in the new Garden.

A singular opportunity of adulthood, for individuals, for nations, and for humanity, is to move beyond the persistent and sad assumption that we can fulfill our true needs by mechanical, formulaic, manipulative means, and discover *in practice* that our genuine wants are finally fulfilled through intensive, principled application of the laws governing creativity — which is precisely the same as saying that an actual want is fulfilled through an act of creative faith. It does not matter that we are not very good at this visionary process of creating — at retaining a tough-minded faith in the result and cultivating Robert Fritz's "structural tension" — when we first consciously attempt it, or, for that matter, even after some period of apprenticeship. (The other night, when for the hundredth time I revealed my own imperfect mastery of the creativity-based approach in the area of domestic finance, my wife kindly remonstrated with me by pointing out that a) my behavior was contradictory to my own principles, b) this did not make me a bad person, just a contradictory one, and

c) somehow we have always managed to get by.) The universe is, at last, infinitely supportive of people who are committed to goals that are worthy of them.

This is not some cotton-candy claim of faux–New Age soft-think, but a fundamental creative principle that had been around for a good while before Goethe remarked on it in the last century. In *The Scottish Himalayan Expedition* (1951), W. H. Murray introduces the Goethe couplet on boldness (the one I quoted in Chapter 4) with these words:

> Concerning all acts of initiative (and creation), there is one elementary truth, the ignorance of which kills count-less ideas and splendid plans: that the moment one defi-nitely commits oneself, then Providence moves too. All sorts of things occur to help one that would never other-wise have occurred. A whole stream of events issues from the decision, raising in one's favour all manner of unfore-seen incidents and meetings and material assistance, which no man could have dreamt would have come his way.

It greatly tests the mettle of individuals and organizations to give this wonderful-sounding notion something deeper than lip service. That is doubly true, for those of us laboring in the vine-yards of environmental and social improvement, when it comes to the business of spreading word of our activities and conveying to the public the reasons we deem them necessary in the first place.

For almost ten years I served as an activist, and as a sort of roving mouthpiece and explicator, for Greenpeace. The chain of events that brought me to that work (and later brought me to the writing of this book) is utterly and incontrovertibly illustrative of Murray's and Goethe's theme.

When I first made a personal commitment to the activist/ spokesman career at Greenpeace — about two years before being hired by the group — the job did not exist. In fact, unbeknownst to me, Greenpeace at that time had deliberately abandoned the practice that was later to be the bulk of my visible work for the organization, lecturing at colleges and universities. Difficulties in fulfilling its commitment to a previous speaking program and difficulties in finding high-integrity representation through an effective lecture agency led to the old program's termination. In 1985, when I was emerging from intensive studies in how to apply creativity in "real life" and made a specific private commitment (from a sense of personal guidance and under some pressure from a wise friend) to become "a spokesperson for a major environmental organization" — and determined that the organization should be Greenpeace — Greenpeace was ostensibly engaged in the business of making such an outcome highly improbable. It may have been just as well that I was unaware of that outwardly discouraging fact.

In hindsight, it seems to me that Greenpeace was unconsciously clearing the decks in a way that ultimately allowed the creation of something entirely new. It is a basic requisite of the creative process that old systems, if their time is truly past, be dismantled and a space be made for that which awaits birth. When we are engaged in or attached to the old systems, it is challenging to recognize that their time may have gone by; it also requires great insight and intuition on the part of those doing the dismantling to know when it is really necessary and when it may be premature or even downright mistaken.

The sequence of events by which the (apparent) flow of events was reversed contained elements of the superficially bizarre. It included the temporary replacement of a Greenpeace department head with a person who happened to be receptive to the idea of creating a position specifically dedicated to public speaking; the timely involvement of a well-respected lecture agent, David Rich (now of Strategic Events International), in arranging Greenpeace speaking engagements in the Northeast, and his timely approach to the new department head on the subject of creating a national program; my presence in Greenpeace's regional office in Boston at the right moment; and the timing of all the above such that the outgoing executive director for the United States (Steve Sawyer, who moved on to become head of Greenpeace International) was still on the scene to approve both the project and my hiring.

Perhaps the most unusual element, though, is the existence of a letter I'd written to David Rich two or three years previously, which I had forgotten I'd written and he had forgotten he'd received. In that letter (which followed some telephone calls on the subject of David arranging bookings for my one-man show on Thoreau) I'd stated that I had become more interested in traveling to colleges to speak about environmental issues from the perspective of creativity than in touring the campuses of America as a performer. Nowhere in the note, however, did I mention Greenpeace, and we had no further contact at that time.

I had thus written a letter predicting my own future, addressed to perhaps the one individual of my acquaintance whose professional universe would later intersect both mine and that of Greenpeace. He then facilitated a critical connection between those universes without the slightest conscious intent to create the linkage. He did not even know that I had gone to work for Greenpeace in the interim. When he was informed that I had been hired as Greenpeace's new principal speaker, and when I was informed that he was our primary liaison at the agency, the news was startling to both of us. At a later date, this reaction gave way to astonishment when I suddenly remembered the letter and David Rich recalled that he had in fact received it. Goethe and Murray would have been amused.

This personal (and, if you must, anecdotal) evidence bears on the specific subject of this chapter to the extent that my work promoted public awareness of Greenpeace, included media interviews, and received intermittent media coverage (I was for most of my tenure attached to Greenpeace's U.S. media and communications division). The creation of my job and my being hired into the position, combined with the success of the speaking program through its first several years, had some effect on Greenpeace's media profile and its public image. The process by which the position was created and filled, and generated positive results, therefore has some potential value as a model and a suggestion of what is possible in the larger area of public outreach.[1]

I am suggesting that such a confluence of events is readily available to others. I have earlier implied, and now state explicitly, that a parallel result is especially within reach of *anyone who has made a core commitment to a worthy mission in life.* And I am saying that parallel results, in the broad arena of publicity and public relations, are readily and limitlessly available to any organization that commits itself to mastering the creative process, fully invests itself in cultivating structural tension, and passes over manipulative and formulaic approaches to gaining the public's attention in favor of an actual openness to intuition, inspiration, and a larger associative reality.

There was a great measure of faith involved in the founding of Greenpeace, a great willingness to live with uncertainty and, God knows, to live with unpredictability. (A significant, residual strain of that attitude has persisted within the organization to the present day.) It is an example worth study. That inaugural faith has served Greenpeace better than most know or understand, and one of the ways in which it has served has been to draw as if by magnetism a great many individuals, within the media and beyond it, who have assisted in publicizing the group's cause and its work on behalf of that cause — starting with the uniquely perceptive Robert Hunter, who sailed on the initial Greenpeace antinuclear protest voyage as an alternative journalist and then stayed around to join the organization and become one of the leading lights of its early days.

It in no way diminishes the talents, nor demeans the long hard hours of work of my former Greenpeace media colleagues, to say that their efforts have been empowered or lifted up by that large acceptance of uncertainty and by a shared commitment extending forward over twenty-five years from a church basement in British Columbia. It does, however, hold a cautionary note for the organization (and others like it), which today has much more at risk materially and periodically evidences a preoccupation with self-protection and self-perpetuation. A visionary institution survives in the long term not by focusing on survival and survival techniques, but by an absolute investment in creating that which is utterly new and a dedication to mastering the creative process.[2] The keepers of a flame, even if historically successful, are wise to consciously seek out new and better ways to fulfill their charge — and to ignite new and enduring offspring of that flame.

The paradigm for Greenpeace's interaction with the media was established at its inception, during the 1971 antinuclear protest voyage of the chartered *Phyllis Cormack* (aka the *Greenpeace*) toward the American underground nuclear test site at Amchitka Island, in the Aleutian chain. The concept that evolved during that voyage remains instructive today. Credit for defining the paradigm goes to Robert Hunter, who built on the ideas of Marshall McLuhan and came up with the concept of "mind bombs" — ideas and images planted in the public consciousness, through the media, that would ultimately transcend their literal significance so powerfully as to stimulate the transformation of that consciousness.

Hunter knew intuitively that the image of Greenpeace as David to various Goliaths was one that had the potential to yield such a result. On that autumn voyage, the picture of the tiny, venerable, and none-too-seaworthy fishing boat laboring across the stormy Gulf of Alaska toward an uncertain fate (with the un-fullfilled intention of anchoring next to the test site), bearing a crew quite willing to risk their lives on behalf of a peaceful future sans nuclear weaponry, brought the image of Greenpeace to the borders of the mythic in the minds of those who heard and read Hunter's dispatches. Hunter, like most of those aboard, was an original and was given to "original perceptions" (to lift one more phrase from Thoreau), by which I mean that he could periodically hear the wisdom of his genius above the often formulaic tintinnabulations of the rational mind and the distractions of the ego. When it came to dreaming up new concepts for engaging mass consciousness, he was a natural.

It is probably time to find a new name for the phenomenon of the "mind bomb," as the present label is archetypally masculine, deliberately dramatic, and implicitly conflict-based and thus at odds with my intense belief that a mature and creative activism will employ the *language* of creativity along with its principles. Hunter's core concept, though, is timeless. It is the notion of planting a seed in the minds of the individual and the collective culture, a seed that may germinate invisibly and unknown to the bearer and give rise to a thoughtform that in time connects with and stimulates entire, perhaps forgotten, benevolent regions of creative consciousness.

The planting of negative images is the shadow side of this approach. In a Graceful universe even this may be turned toward useful ends, as in the case of the "Doomsday Clock" warning of the potential for nuclear conflict. Or, if employed with sufficient wit, inventiveness, and intelligence — as with one legendary environmentalist banner giving the illusion of a crack in Glen Canyon Dam — a negative image may effectively defuse its own negativity. The greatest challenge, however, lies in bringing forth positive images and positive concepts which through an inherent connection to the mythic (or a resonance with other deeply generative areas of consciousness) stimulate the individual and the culture to go beyond themselves and take constructive action in this world.

One of the rather significant challenges for an organization that positions itself in or near the realm of the mythic is to live up to the self-magnifying image it creates for itself. In one in-house dispatch, Greenpeace U.S. executive director Barbara Dudley raised this point, going so far as to state that "Greenpeace is a myth created by the public" whose criteria for this status the group must constantly strive to meet. I would agree conditionally, making the case that a) Greenpeace activists inaugurated the Greenpeace legend themselves, and have guided its evolution over the years *in cooperation* with the public, and b) the Greenpeace "myth" is one well-rooted in both material and higher realities, since the group has continued to do its work on the ethical basis established twenty-five years ago, and with demonstrable impact. (I obviously have no quarrel with Barbara Dudley's sense that it is daily required that the organization actually maintain a very, very high standard, one which lifts it significantly above the mundane and the routine in the minds of its fellow citizens of the planet; it is precisely that sense which has constituted one major impetus in the writing of this book.)

However, if you are going to invest your spirit, your time, your energy, and your (benefactors') money in living up to a myth, it is singularly important to choose the right myth to live up to. The David-and-Goliath imagery is technically still quite applicable not only to Greenpeace, but to nearly every legitimate activist entity on the planet. (Greenpeace's former U.S. media director, Peter Dykstra, now at CNN, used to like to point out that General Motors spends the equivalent of Greenpeace's entire annual budget every few hours.) Yet Greenpeace, like a few other visionary organizations, has established itself so firmly in mass consciousness and acquired so large a reputation that it may need to consciously cultivate a new mythos. Seeding the public consciousness this time around would likely require some different material means (though it would surely involve an engagement of the media); the underlying process, however, must obey the same laws as did Robert Hunter's in 1971. A major difference in circumstances is that such a group today has the chance to accomplish consciously, and with a more detailed knowledge of the principles involved, what Hunter *et al.* accomplished largely from native ingenuity and native intuition.

As a hypothetical case study, let us examine how Greenpeace or any other activist organization might set such a process effectively in motion. For any group, such a generative process is *least* effectively begun with assumptions about *how* to do it, which is of course the first place most groups, like most individuals, tend to put their focus. In hot pursuit of the familiar, they start with a list of known techniques before clearly establishing the *goal* those techniques are meant to serve. But truly creative organizations begin with little or no interest in technique. They instead begin by cooperatively and collectively envisioning, usually in some colorful detail, the genuinely desirable result: in this case, the establishment of a global focus on the organization and its cause, and the active engagement of millions of souls in that cause. They agree to begin with *absolutely no assumed limitations:* they simply will not, in the words of Cornel West, "allow the present circumstances to dictate [their] conception of the future." But they also begin with an honest and accurate accounting of those present circumstances, good *and* ill, on both visible and invisible levels.[3]

For any environmental organization today, this implies taking time to acknowledge thoughtfully and in some detail the real, transcultural impact of activism since Earth Day 1970, while observing with equal specificity the ways in which public attention to the earth's systems is now largely distracted. This is something rarely done; the ground covered to date is taken as a given, and reviewing it is often seen as a self-indulgent diversion from the "real" work at hand. For Greenpeace, the accounting would demand attention to both the definable advantages of the organization's now-elevated status and the new and strenuous requirements imposed in the last quarter-century — such as rigorous accuracy (where the group fell short in the Brent Spar case) and rigorous honesty (where in that same case it succeeded). Something Robert Fritz makes plain is that only by establishing and bearing with the structural tension between a very clear vision of the desired outcome on the one hand, and a relentlessly accurate accounting of existing circumstances on the other, can we enter fully and *consciously* into the creative process.

Only *after* this vital groundwork is laid does the time come to establish a sequence of tangible or easily identifiable goals to be achieved en route to the larger one, and only at this point might the attention of the media become a specified aim. Media attention is not, after all, a goal of any value whatsoever on its own merits; its value exists entirely in its usefulness to the larger goal of mobilizing public consciousness to worthy ends.

The media has become an instrument of entertainment at the expense of enlightenment in large part because it is unconsciously regarded as an end rather than a means. If I go out and get myself arrested in a highly public fashion by blocking the driveway of the White House, as a symbolic response to the political roadblocks to a healthy environment set up by a myopic president, and if (as has happened) a conventionally dramatic photograph of my arrest is subsequently published in a newspaper, what good does it do me or the planet if those people who see the photograph are caught up in the so-called drama of the event but fail to gain some understanding of why I was there in the first place? One enormous and all-too-frequent frustration for activists has been getting media coverage of one or another highly public demonstration, only to find that reporters have presented the event as the functional equivalent of a circus, with little or no real explanation of the issue which stimulated the protest.

If we want our issues addressed in depth and in an enlightened context, we must begin by maintaining an intensely disciplined sense of that context in our own consciousness. This can be exceptionally challenging to do as you make the hundredth telephone call or send the hundredth fax to an unresponsive news desk, but it is essential. "In the long run," said Thoreau, "men hit only what they aim at." The results we obtain finally reflect where our consciousness has been primarily or dominantly focused. There is no more bedrock principle than this in all real teaching of the creative process.

"Getting the message through" is never more than a secondary, or tertiary, or quaternary, goal. The power informing any great process comes not from the process itself, but from the greatness of an overriding vision of transformation in this world. It rests in the ultimate and enlightened What, never in the momentary mechanical How. Functional mastery of this truth allows one to draw greatness out of others who may or may not have demonstrated it previously. If we want the media to become what most of us say we want it to be, we have to guard against the feeling that the media inevitably defines itself. It finally responds to the dominant paradigm in mass consciousness. For many reasons, activists worthy of the title have a particular influence on that paradigm. One avenue of influence is the way we regard the media when we are trying to employ its services.

Chapter Twelve

The Coming Generation
of Creators

For over a decade, the principal focus of my professional life has been speaking to students, primarily at colleges and universities, but also at every educational level from preschool through high school.

In that period, I have seen campus interest in and awareness of environmental issues in America rise to an all-time high at the twentieth anniversary of Earth Day in 1990, and fall to a benchmark low some six years later. The reasons generally cited pertain to the state of the country's economy, to student preoccupation with jobs and careers to the exclusion of social issues, and the national shift away from issues identified — however shortsightedly — with a liberal agenda.

Such swings of the cultural pendulum are an actual phenomenon, and their existence must be acknowledged. They can, however, be transcended by those individuals and organizations with sufficient mastery of events to live and move beyond the pendulum's mechanics. The principles outlined in this book are those recognized as fundamental by people who have the capacity to bring events to them, rather than waiting to be carried forward by events.

Knowledge and awareness of these principles is more readily available to people in this culture today than at any other time, or in any other culture, in human history. If we are to not merely survive but more auspiciously fulfill our destiny here as a uniquely gifted and creative species, a great many more of us will need to gain mastery of these principles and demonstrate that mastery in the progress of our individual lives and careers.

One of the most important places to begin this process of cultural renaissance is in our educational institutions, at every level, by making principles of creativity, and an activist ethic, readily available to coming generations. The number of deeply creative souls in this culture is extraordinarily high (whence come, for example, our phenomenal advances in such fields as computer technology and many related areas of applied science). It is a tragedy when anyone is programmed to believe that her or his creative gifts must be "packaged" in ways that limit their fulfillment. Such programming begins when people are very, very young; our schools and colleges have a singular opportunity to replace it with messages that are deeply positive. In a world where it is already becoming an accepted assumption that the average individual will go through some seven major job and career changes, we should be emphasizing that the point of all this transition is to become the master of your own destiny, not the passive object of an increasing number of external forces — and that one's true destiny always involves becoming a benefactor of the world, not an increasingly sophisticated net consumer of its material resources and opportunities.

We should be teaching art, in its largest sense, to students at every level. And we should be doing it in a way which makes utterly clear that great art is always activist in the highest meaning of the term.

* * *

Several years ago I was part of a committee that tried to draft a program that would help Greenpeace effectively reach out to and inspire young people in America. Our counterparts in Germany and one or two other European countries had already established successful programs, and we wanted to see whether we could come up with something workable, with minimal financial resources available and a minimum of personnel, for a country so much larger.

This is not the place to discuss the frustrations of committee life within a nonprofit organization (rendered the more intense because the committee met almost exclusively by telephone). Suffice it to say that by the end of our tenure several of us felt that any one of us working alone might well have accomplished more than the group did. Despite the frustration, I for one got an unexpected and useful education from the experience. In addition to having spoken to thousands of students in my travels, I had once been a teacher at the secondary school level and had long been of the opinion that Greenpeace should make interaction with schools and students a greater priority. The committee's discussions, however outwardly unproductive, obliged me to focus my thoughts on the subject in a way I had not done previously.

At one point in our deliberations, I drafted a proposal for a basic structure that we would be able to offer to schools requesting ideas for an environmental program, as envisioned from our activist perspective. The proposal was passed over by the committee, but I found drafting it worth my time and effort. Designed to allow a school to "flesh out" its own program in its own way—not an exhaustive curriculum, but rather a guide—it remains for me a suggestion of how basic creative principles might be incorporated in a program that could be broadly acceptable and easily adapted to different educational levels and different circumstances. It was also designed as something that could be made available literally for the cost of printing up the outline.

The basic steps it suggested for educators — which I have here adapted slightly to embrace curriculums going beyond "green" or ecological issues alone — were these:

1) *Before doing anything else, have students create an environment.* Highly recommended choices are a garden, a greenhouse, and/or a botanical center.[1] Green plants must be an element of the environment, which can also include explorations of such areas as geology, architecture, landscape architecture, and beyond. (A curriculum focusing on issues of peace and justice, for example, might imply the creation of an environment akin or analagous to that of a Zen monastery garden.) A commitment should be made to tend and enhance this environment for the duration of the project — and usually beyond.

   It would be difficult to overstate the importance of this foundational step — and it is hard to imagine how one could spend too much time on it during the run of the project. Something to which the students can return regularly (and preferably at their own discretion) throughout the program, such an environment focuses their positive, creative, and nurturing abilities. It has the potential to serve as both laboratory and sanctuary. Its simple, essential premise is that activism needs a strong positive and creative base if it is to be sustained over a long term, and that those individuals who remain committed to activism draw constantly from an inner reservoir of faith and confidence in their ability to make things better, not just stave off human-induced disasters. Something along these lines was incorporated in the American end of a small-scale experimental U.S.-European-Russian Greenpeace curriculum in 1989–90, known as the East-West Program.

2) *Identify a range of local social and/or environmental issues.* Specific local concerns that afford a clear opportunity for the students to assess a situation, express their opinions, and have an impact on the outcome are best. Obviously, issues should be chosen that can be grasped easily by the students at each particular grade level. This approach, along with step 5, below, was also used by the East-West program staff.

3) *Identify positive models.* Find successful local activists, writers, artists, photographers, journalists, entrepreneurs, and/or businesses with an exceptional commitment to the health of society and the environment; find local government officials with an equally outstanding commitment; identify other local individuals who embody a healthy, effective orientation toward life and toward the planet; search out local programs that have successfully addressed social and environmental needs.

Make contact with as many of these individuals and organizations as you can. Ask as many as possible to come and discuss their experiences. Rather than putting any of them on a pedestal, explore how their forms of activism may suggest that similar avenues are available to others.

4) *Identify global issues.* Offer an overview of the most important issues of the day (for example, global peace issues, matters of international free trade and economic equity, global warming, ozone layer depletion, temperate and rainforest destruction, gross pollution of air, water, and soil). The overview should be a simplified, easily understandable presentation which should avoid technical detail and should *avoid dramatization of the negative,* especially of imagined negative outcomes. It should make any natural linear connections with local issues, but not force them. The potential for *associative* connections between local and global issues — for example, for developing momentum throughout the culture through the actions of small, seemingly isolated activities — should be underscored.

5) *Select a local issue (or issues) for action.* Ensure that any issue chosen is workable for the student age level(s) involved. That is, the students must be able to clearly understand the nature of each issue, they must see what stake they have in any outcomes, and there must be the genuine opportunity for making a successful contribution to a desirable result. The students must have a major say (even *the* major say) in the choice of issues; it may be best to offer a range of possibilities, allowing the group to make choices as individuals or subgroups.

6) *Clearly identify a consensual vision of a desired, ideal, long-term outcome(s).* It is strongly recommended that the students explore the highest goals they can conceive of (as modeled, for example, in many activists' insistence on the total elimination of nuclear weapons, or in Greenpeace's

ultimate commitment to zero discharge of industrial toxics into the environment — though the goal should be
stated first in the positive: "a world at peace, with no
nuclear weapons"). Emphasize long-term commitment
above short-term gratification — without ever ruling out
the latter as a simultaneous possibility.

If the scope of the vision goes well beyond the local issue, so be it — the students can define a local vision to
complement the larger one. Use formal visualization
techniques to reinforce the group commitment to the
long-term goal — everything from brief, closed-eye visualization techniques to positive art/photographic images,
preferably images created by the students themselves. Visualize the positive — the presence of what *is* wanted, not
just the absence of what isn't.

7) *Strategize imaginatively.* Without the students' concern-
ing themselves initially with rationally generated estimates of probabilities of success, map out several conceivable courses to the desired result(s), being receptive to
both rational *and* intuitive suggestions from all participants. Don't discard unusual or "impossible" plans without discussion; operate by consensus wherever possible.
Look for strategies that engage the group fully and offer
roles for all its members. Broadly, these might include
documenting the situation (locating existing evidence
and/or generating new evidence), publicizing it, addressing it, and following up to ensure that results are
lasting.

8) *Take initial action.* In line with a consensual strategy, take
the first necessary step (or, if no one step takes clear prece-

dence, take the one agreed at by consensus). This will almost always involve documenting the situation you plan
to address (unless *complete* documentation was done in
steps 2 and 5). There is particular room for creativity
here, from employing the talents of student artists, map-
makers and journalists to using school-owned audiovisual
equipment for interviews and commentaries.

9) *Renew your vision.* Make sure that the vision (and the
group's commitment to it) is holding up in the face of a
detailed awareness of the challenges faced. Rather than
abandoning a worthwhile vision in the face of an informed recognition of the obstacles, try to recommit as
long as the goal still seems worthwhile.

10) *Promote your cause.* Find the most powerful method of
publicizing the issue you can, suitable for the age and
grade level of the students involved. Be alert to inspiration and a sense of new or unusual methods that might
serve your efforts. Use those means that afford an opportunity for the expression of conscience as agreed on by
consensus.

11) *Measure your progress.* Decide which "barometers" of
progress (from the level of group fulfillment to the number of people reached, the extent of media coverage, legis-
lative results, etc.) are most valuable, and focus on them.
Reassess your strategies in light of this review.

12) *Celebrate all significant positive results.* Find creative ways
to acknowledge the effectiveness of the group — and celebrate *both* those results directly connected to the group's
efforts (linear progress) *and* those that may not appear to
be connected (which can represent associative progress;

do not ignore "coincidences"). Note that "significant" is not used here as a synonym for "large" — observe small significant results as well, and celebrate them with equal gusto.

13) *Repeat steps 7 through 12 as needed.*

To be successful, any such program for young people must develop and exercise both individual and collective creativity, as well as the deeply related phenomenon of individual conscience, as spurs to the kind of positive action that will shape a better world. It is essential that we focus on activism as a fundamentally creative, positive, and proactive process, in which problem solving is secondary to the artistic, visionary, grounded process of making the world healthy, sane, and joyful.[2]

The world does not need yet another educational program for young citizens based on the concept that there have always been problems, there are now unspeakable problems, and there will presumably always be problems. Aside from leaving a negative residue in one's consciousness, such an approach yields an unsettlingly high percentage of program graduates who are, de facto, addicted to the existence of dandy problems to solve. Meanwhile, it tends to come up short in the fairly significant area of generating visionaries, true leaders, and determined artists. If we want to create a renewed planet, we need to inspire and train creators.

I would also note that any program in global citizenship will find itself welcomed by potential sponsors and participants with an effusiveness directly proportionate to its emphasis on the *possibility of creating a healthy planet*. People like to hear that dreams can come true, even if your message also contains the less comfortable truth that they may have to work hard before it happens. During the years of the Greenpeace college speaking program, sponsors — often anxious about the possibility of bringing onto their campuses someone who might depress an entire student audience — were pleased to discover that I was in fact focused on the continuing opportunity to improve things.

Greenpeace's reports on the existing state of the world, like those of other respected organizations, from Worldwatch to the Southern Poverty Law Center to the Children's Defense Fund, are highly rated by various authorities for their accuracy. They tend — unless presented melodramatically — to speak for themselves; despondency on the part of the hearer remains optional. And Greenpeace's report that it is still possible to shape a happy destiny for ourselves, individually and collectively, along with our report on the technological (and philosophical) components of that destiny, was universally welcomed by the audiences I addressed on the group's behalf. The same response will greet that message from the lips of any speaker whose audience perceives her or him to be genuine.

If my experience is any barometer, it will also greet reflections on the importance of an individual's mission or calling in life, the opportunity and significance of viewing oneself as an artist (something I've often referred to from the lectern as "the great human birthright"), the overarching vision of the planet as an individual and collective work of art, and the paramount opportunity of seeing one's own life as a potentially great work of unique and personal art. All of the above are cross-cultural principles that can be grasped by a diverse student body anywhere in the United States, and presumably elsewhere with some adaptation.

Beyond the matter of promoting creativity, the matter of promoting conscience — and more particularly, acts of conscience — poses interesting challenges. There are numerous venues (most public schools, many homes and families) that are hardly yet prepared to allow explicit encouragement of civil disobedience among young people, but virtually all schools and sponsors accept the concept of an *appeal* to conscience. And almost any potential sponsor will be tolerant of an explanation of an activist philosophy that is an extension of the thinking of the Society of Friends and of Henry David Thoreau, of Mahatma Gandhi and of Martin Luther King, Jr., and of numerous other persons who have shared the perception that the nonviolent bearing of witness is a long-term, practicable, and conscientious means to change human society for the better.

In this country, within the dominant culture and to a large extent beyond it, it is worth noting that both Thoreau and Dr. King have become cultural icons. Their principled reflections and actions have established clear precedents which are by now accepted and reverenced by credible educators. Yet the primary implication of these precedents — the need for conscientious *acts* by individuals — is still largely unexplored by a great many of these same educators, and thus by their young clientele. A pivotal opportunity therefore exists for any inspirational and educational activist program to provoke in both educators and students, gently yet firmly, a genuine examination of this need. In short, we must prepare and inspire people of *all* ages to make some rather dramatic choices, not just admire other people for making them.

Finally, if it is the intention of activists to promote a philosophy derived from that of Gandhi and other great teachers, I would submit that the personnel of an activist organization who present such an inspirational/educational program to educators — and all the more so if they are presenting directly to the students — need to be willing to take part in the kind of direct action such a philosophy recommends. Note that I say *willing* to take part; I stop short of demanding a prior individual history of protests, confrontations, arrests, and associated occurrences. I require the willingness, at a minimum, partly because I am convinced that one of the most significant elements in the success of my own work was my insistence, when hired as a Greenpeace spokesperson, that I be allowed to take part in the activities I was hired to speak about.[3] I believe it is remarkably difficult to stand before even (or especially!) a third-grade class and present the concept of "acts of conscience" unless one is prepared to embody such a creed. It is not just a matter of being able to "speak from experience"; we carry with us an intangible aura that reveals the level and intensity of our commitment to the principles we claim to endorse.

I understand that not everyone is enthusiastic about the idea of standing in the way of harpoons, blocking governmental driveways, dangling from assorted smokestacks, or levitating oneself up the face of various federal, state, or corporate facilities. As someone who once never expected to take part in such pursuits, I can sympathize heartily with this point of view. Furthermore, there are a great many opportunities in this world for people to embody a philosophy of nonviolent direct intervention in less visible or conventionally dramatic ways than those noted above. Yet I perceive that a great many people who are activists at heart are missing a unique and genuinely joyful, if admittedly stress-inducing, opportunity by foreclosing such an option for themselves. And I have a reluctance to send into classrooms, lecture halls, or (for that matter) boardrooms any inspirational/educational activist representative who is not prepared to embody the philosophy for which the greatest activists are known and respected.

The applicability of the program outlined above is hardly limited to the efforts of educators and their students. Most of its procedures are regularly carried out by activists at every level of experience. Others, however, such as the unfettered exploration of imaginative strategies (including the nominally outrageous), the formal use of visualization to the end of arriving at a genuine vision, and the acknowledgment of potential associative connections between actions and results, are pathetically rare. Among the most notable and regrettable exclusions is the first step — the hands-on creation of an original environment. This leads me to speculate that any professional environmental group which does not at a minimum have a greenhouse on its premises is slightly suspect (and I take the essence of this thought, at least, with a good deal of seriousness).

In most people the generative instinct is less clamorous than the instinct to fix what appears broken, rescue what appears threatened, and save what seems about to be lost. Yet creators are thoroughly familiar with the seeming paradox that we accomplish all of these things better, more easily, and often without even particularly noticing it, when we are engaged *primarily* in acts of creation.

Chapter Thirteen

Creativity, Compassion, and Mission

Hanging on the door of our refrigerator, and on that of at least one other spiritual revolutionary I know, is a quotation from writer and speaker Marianne Williamson. It begins thus:

> Our deepest fear is not that we are inadequate. Our deepest fear is that we are powerful beyond measure.[1]

I was struck by this statement when I first encountered it, for several reasons. For one thing, I had once heard the case made by Robert Fritz that many individuals who resort to suicide do so, on the deepest level, not because of despair, nor because at bottom they believe themselves incapable of altering their circumstances, but rather because they are unconsciously afraid that the full exercise of their spirits in this world will injure others. The implications of this idea for activism, and perhaps especially for those who might become activists but have not made the choice to do so, are profound.

At first glance, the above quotation would not seem to apply to many serious reformers. People who make a career of activism, or, for that matter, even people whose careers are activist only in one particular aspect, are often regarded as a hard-nosed bunch. There is a reasonable amount of truth in this stereotype. I have even heard one or two colleagues, no shrinking violets

themselves, express some surprise at the degree to which toughness was valued in their respective organizations. Generally
speaking, the activist world is dominated by people who are not
greatly alarmed at the prospect of upsetting the applecarts of
others, at least when the applecarts appear to stand directly in
the way of needed social progress. And yet even revolutionary
souls may impose limits on themselves. I have witnessed a fair
number of my outwardly radical compatriots reject radical opportunities to learn new ways of expressing their innermost
strengths.

Further, we would have the company of a good many more
souls in the activist ranks if we made a little more room for
people who do not initially think of themselves as powerful. It
might help if it were better understood that there are different
forms of toughness. It is not a one-size-fits-all proposition.

In my own case, I was surely drawn to Greenpeace to reduce
the disparity between a personality which (like that of most per-
formers) did not historically thrive on confrontation, and my
spirit, which as best I can make out would be pleased to take on
all available adversaries before lunchtime. By placing myself in
an environment where confrontation would be a more or less
regular aspect of existence, I intuitively knew there was an opportunity for my personality to become less oversensitive and
more persistent in matters of real significance. (The converse of
this was that I could present the organization's view of things,
through the filter of that same personality, in a way that made
our perspective accessible to many people who might well have
dismissed some of my colleagues, however unwisely, as zealots.)

The kind of toughness I have most respected is therefore a
kind of durability rather than an intense assertiveness, or ag-

gressiveness. These latter qualities have their place in the mix of things, and no activist can accomplish great ends without the ability to assert herself or himself when the occasion calls for it — the trick being to recognize when the occasion does call for it and when it does not. Still, the greatest prerequisite for activists is staying power. Having asserted oneself on an issue of significance to the well-being of future generations, it is essential to remain engaged long enough to accomplish something tangible. Even where results may be generated quickly (and it does happen), the intensity of the process generally requires a certain sturdiness of soul to deal with the turbulence that may be thrown up. Creativity requires some healthy tolerance for creative stress, all the more so at the level where you are trying to create a world.

I associate the toughness of durability specifically with certain qualities of the heart, and it is those activists whose hearts remain simultaneously resilient and open whom I most appreciate and admire. Such individuals have the remarkable and all too rare ability to promote the long-term welfare of others, and of the planet, without losing an awareness of their short-term welfare. They are able to help others see past their immediate fears and anxieties (such as the culture-wide anxiety about trading off economic stability for environmental well-being) long enough to focus on the long term.

If you accept the idea that treating your own emotional demands (such as the desire for predictability and comfort) as a top priority constitutes a short-term investment at best, and if you believe as I do that emotions are the "shifting sands" referred to in the New Testament parable of the house unwisely built, and if you would nevertheless like to minimize the emotional turbulence for other human beings confronted with the necessity of transformation, all this raises important questions about the real nature of compassion. Judged relative to the long-term welfare of an individual's spirit, and of the planet, compassion appears one way; judged more conventionally and relative to an individual's feelings, it may appear quite differently.

These dichotomous views of compassion are analagous to the old activist parable of teaching someone to fish as opposed to giving him a fish to eat. But, to strain the analogy a little, one does not wish the nascent fisherman to go hungry, or worse, before he has mastered the new skill. Activists may rightly judge that great changes are needed in society, and in the lives of individuals, if we and the planet are to progress and indeed to endure. But what is our responsibility for easing the transition into a new phase, particularly when the "new phase" begins to look more and more like a radical metamorphosis?

There has been a learning process in this matter for many groups and individuals. When a smaller, younger, less experienced, but very earnest (and still primarily Canadian) Greenpeace first ventured onto the pack ice off Newfoundland in 1976 to protest the massive commercial slaughter of baby harp seals, it had no proposal in hand for an alternative economy for the local seal hunters. After some intense and educational exchanges with the communities ashore, the group backpedaled and limited the target of its protests to the large-scale hunts carried out from ships by hunters from Canada and Norway; it publicly made a distinction between those operations and the hunting by local sealers, which was essentially a subsistence enterprise. But a good deal of damage had been done, and there are places in eastern Canada today where the mention of the name Green-peace still awakens the old controversy and opens old wounds.

It is improbable that the Greenpeace of today would venture any such campaign without a) a far greater understanding of its implications, especially its economic and social implications for a local population without evident recourse to alternatives, and b) a well-mapped strategy for making at least some partial alternative available, and publicizing it. This change is no public relations ploy, but evidence that, the opinions of some critics to the contrary, activists do learn from their experience — and most of them do not wish ill even to their apparent and most immediate adversaries.

It is a fundamental task of activists to accurately perceive the long-term needs of a culture and to take a stand for them. This means bearing witness to what is wanted, in the deepest sense, for the health of the individual and the health of society. The principle of "no separation" applies: the individual suffers when the culture is wounded, even if the consequences to the individual are masked in the near term. Yet there has to be a place for some compassionate alleviation of short-term pain, or individuals may reject the larger lessons at hand and sacrifice parts of the future for the sake of avoiding the immediate discomfort that accompanies these lessons. A compassion based only in sentiment is insufficient; actions based on sentimental compassion alone tend to undermine, not further, a vision. Dealing with the implications, for affected individuals and populations, of a long-term investment in the welfare of the whole therefore requires a challenging, transsentimental mastery of the creative process.

Today a group like Greenpeace has to confront the impact of its campaigns on millions of people, for example, people who will be affected by the demise of industrial uses of chlorine — a major Greenpeace campaign goal (with increasing scientific and even political support) because of the implication of chlorinated organic pollutants in cancer, birth defects, and other major public health problems. The organization has therefore become increasingly adept, and more intense, in its pursuit of demonstrable alternatives to those existing technologies that are debilitating to society and to the welfare of individuals. (For instance, the group has aggressively promoted TCF — totally chlorine-free — bleaching of pulp and paper; it has widely publicized the existence of nontoxic drycleaning methods; and, in 1996, it organized an unprecedented international conference of major potential investors in solar technologies.)

Something Greenpeace has *not* done, on the other hand, is take time to routinely and formally *envision positive outcomes* — deliberately, compassionately, and as a discipline — *especially ones specific to those individuals who are our visible antagonists.* We had, during my tenure, endless discussions of adversarial strategies and tactics, but almost never discussions (much less meditations) on the possibilities of the transformation of relationship — because we have been culturally programmed to regard such imaginative exercises as "unrealistic."

I expect that this criticism will anger some people, who will maintain that they do not have the time to spend in such seemingly esoteric pursuits as visualization, or visionary meditation. But I aim the criticism at myself as much as, or more than, at others. In truth, it says something about an immaturity of our whole culture that such an exercise strikes most of us as an imposition rather than an opportunity. My airplane encounter with the Arco executive suggests a possibility — and a responsibility — in our work that few activists have grasped. We should treat the powerful process of envisioning outcomes formally and with respect. And our visions, starting with the conscious visualizations that may lead us to a far greater pictography of the spirit, should be deeply inclusive.

If such a possibility is to be brought to fruition, it becomes essential to grasp the distinction between a compassion that is merely sentimental and a more powerful compassion that is truly creative. This distinction rests in part on such abilities as genuine intuition, which can enable one to sense when a well-intentioned act will really promote another's welfare and when it will not. Considering the old Boy Scout model which prescribed helping elderly persons across metropolitan streets, one notes that such a gesture becomes a long-term liability if the person assisted then arrives at the next street crossing just in time to get hit by an oncoming vehicle. An actual (not a wishful) intuition allows one to know when a compassionate gesture is really compassionate and when it finally amounts to interference. An act that is kindly intended but short-circuits a vital learning process for the recipient is less than kind in the end. Learning to make such distinctions is a fairly high art.

An equally high, and related, art is that of true compromise, which also should have everything to do with accurately assessing long-term needs. Thanks largely to the machinations of irresolute politicians, the very word "compromise" has taken on a sickly hue. Political compromises are rarely creative in a real sense; rather they tend to the corrosive, consisting of arrangements in which some type of quid pro quo is negotiated in which nobody really gets what they want, and in which the public interest and the long-term view are barely discernable as influences. But the Latin roots of the word imply a joint commitment to an arbitrated settlement. Compromise in its original sense does not inherently imply any imposed limitation on any worthwhile vision; to the contrary, it appeals to an objective third party to ascertain what is best for all concerned. Such a genuinely disinterested arbitrator would be perfectly free to hand down a decision which took as its first principle the long-term welfare of all affected parties.

A creative compromise is one in which none of the worthy goals of any party are eroded or bargained away. It is one in which the parties, after objective review, discover mutual interests, discard those elements that are, in truth, not really wanted because they are not for the highest good, and refine their vision in accord with the highest common welfare, not the lowest common material or psychological denominator. This is hard work. It is made far easier if the parties are sufficiently intuitive and perceptive to sense where each other's best and highest interests really lie, and sufficiently honest to acknowledge what their own best interests really are, especially when the party on the other side of the table makes a legitimate suggestion or recommendation. And its rewards can be very great indeed. Among the most gratifying is the occasional discovery that at bottom the parties involved actually want the same thing.

This approach to compromise is based in what I would call the doctrine of simultaneous gain, rather than in the more conventional credo which has become routine in political life. *That* cancerous methodology, which has damaged citizens' trust in the institutions of government around the globe, is generally based instead in a doctrine of mutual loss. The human spirit instinctively knows such a process to be corrosive. It is up to individual human beings to guard against the tendency to indulge in it. It is largely up to activist organizations to block this tendency in its collective form at every available turn.

Compassion enters into the process of legitimate compromise wherever the parties involved commit themselves to enhancing both long-term *and* short-term welfare, even while the first priority is still a refusal to pursue the latter at the former's expense. And compassion becomes visionary and deeply transformative when the parties are each willing to accept discomfort on behalf of the welfare of the other. Few challenges to the visionary individual are greater than rendering a vision so unselfish that it literally embraces the welfare of an adversary while simultaneously holding out the possibility that one's adversary might make a similar commitment. Yet there are people who manage to do both these things.

Certainly the Dalai Lama and those around him do so; few phenomena of modern diplomacy, and ethics, are more striking than the Tibetan forbearance toward successive Chinese leaders, to whom an open-ended invitation is offered to negotiate a just and mutually beneficial political arrangement between Tibet and China. In fact, this is a great deal more than forbearance, since it involves the constant and unswerving discipline of holding open a door through which the Chinese leadership could pass at any moment — and keeping it always at least ajar even in the face of deliberate and self-destructive Chinese efforts to force it shut.

Such a discipline as the Tibetans', while admired in the West, is not often seen for what it is. The Western activist is likely to filter awareness of such activities through his or her own preconceptions about the meaning of unselfishness and sacrifice. The latter concept is widely confused with such notions as the hair shirt, and rarely understood in terms of its real origins. Actually, sacrifice simply refers to "doing what is sacred." It involves allegiance to and conscious awareness of a high order of truth. The hair shirt is optional. The unconscious Western misinterpretation is akin or parallel to our misunderstanding of the word "courage," which, far from having its origins in any macho stereotype, is, as I have mentioned, based in that Latin root meaning "heart."

Immature activism clings to a formulaic perfectionism. Erosive politics notwithstanding, activists cannot afford to dismiss the concept of compromise in its real and creative sense; instead, we should busy ourselves with reclaiming the original meaning of the word. Idealism and perfectionism are not the same. Perfectionism impedes both idealism and compassion; it blocks relationship between or among souls. A genuine idealism constantly subjects itself to review and searches out ways to grow ever more inclusive while vigilantly guarding its original essence. It is the *essence* that it protects, not preexisting assumptions about the process by which that essence must be ("perfectly") manifested. True idealism is based in the deepest desire to embrace both the greatest good and the greatest number who may benefit from that good. It looks to the seventh generation, and beyond, while never losing sight of those whom it affects today.

Finding or creating ways of fulfilling long-term needs while simultaneously identifying and satisfying the greatest short-term needs is the essence of an enlightened activism. It requires a willingness to evolve, and to hold, a comprehensive vision — to "dream tough," if you will — even in the face of circumstances that so-called realists would define as prohibitive. Compassion, notably compassion for those affected by the transformational process such a vision sets in motion and *especially* compassion for those who display resistance to the transformation, enlarges and expands the creative process in new dimensions. In this sense, we ultimately gain at least as much from our (nominal) enemies as from our friends and allies.

When one is attempting to create and establish wholly new "ways of doing business" on the planet, and even wholly new ways of thinking, it becomes critical not merely to identify the world's deficiencies, but to clearly identify also every significant step taken by a culture in the direction of creative change. No real progress — I repeat, none — is beneath notice. The greater the existing deficiencies, the more important it is to recognize and appreciate even the *smallest* advance. It is not just a matter of providing encouragement to those who are involved in the process, nor of recruitment, as important as those elements must be. The greatest priority here for a successful activist is to send an accurate message to oneself that one is *having a positive impact*. This is not just a psychological matter; it is a structural one. It's not about breaking your arm patting yourself on the back; it's about clinical acknowledgment of progress. Advances are built on advances.

The art of identifying small advances is of large consequence in the creative process, and it is essential to building momentum. For most people, the process of creating *anything* significant — let alone attempting to transform society in some way — is experienced as rather like turning some great ship, whose wake may offer no encouragingly immediate evidence that the vessel is responding to your hand at the helm.[2] Therefore one does well to appreciate even the most subtle indications — the slight shuddering of the hull as the vessel begins to turn into its own path, the very intensity of the resistance felt through the wheel — that some progress is being made.

A friend once expanded the analogy for me by pointing out that on very large ships, because the rudder itself is so massive, a "tab" is built into it. The action of the helm first turns that tab. Only after this movement is initiated can the rudder itself start to come around, and only then can the vessel come about. The ultimate progress of the ship, then, is actually determined by influencing the motion of a minuscule part of its structure, whose influence will at first be well-nigh imperceptible. This says something about the significance of (seemingly) small actions taken by those who are attempting to turn the ship. When the metaphorical vessel we are talking about is an entire planet and its global "megaculture," the ship is large enough that many people can barely comprehend its size and mass, let alone clearly visualize its ideal course. Even the rudder alone is large enough that many people have considerable difficulty imagining that they might be able to turn the thing and hold it in the necessary position in the face of inertia and resistance. But the *tab*, now . . .

How many people, at the moment of the event, appreciated the significance of Rosa Parks's refusal to go to the back of the bus?

Activists need to learn to value their own contributions rightly and objectively, and we may as well start with certain contributions that we may have been unconsciously programmed to regard as too small or too "ordinary" to be worthy of our attention. We should be extremely suspicious, standing amidst a reality that revels in its own infinite associative possibilities, of our rationally conditioned tendency to say that *any* progress occurs wholly independent of our highest intentions or of even the smallest actions we take on their behalf. Those intentions invite assistance we may barely guess at and which may rightly inspire awe; and those smallest actions that accord with a high intention may release into the world such creative energies as will, in time, transform it utterly.

In the several years since I found my way into the activist universe, a rather significant number of interesting developments have occurred. Among other notable items, in no conscious order of importance, the list includes:

- The signing of an international agreement that protects Antarctica from commercial minerals exploration and exploitation, including drilling for oil and gas, for a minimum of fifty years.
- The convening of the Earth Summit in Rio de Janeiro, and the signing of a global agreement to limit emissions of carbon dioxide, the principal global warming gas.
- The signing of the Montreal Protocol, which phases out the manufacture and use of major ozone-destroying chemicals.
- The successful protest, by the citizens of the low-income Latino farmworking community of Kettleman City, California, of plans by the world's largest waste disposal firm to build one of the world's largest hazardous waste incinerators in their community.
- The passage by two Southern California county boards of

supervisors of resolutions opposing the establishment of a low-level radioactive waste dump in the state.

- The broad institution and acceptance of recycling programs across the United States, with such cumulative nationwide impacts as the recycling of more than 50,000 aluminum cans per minute.

- The election of an American vice president who has written a major, bestselling work on the state of the global environment.

- The dismantling, without violent revolution, of apartheid in South Africa, and the election of Nelson Mandela as president.

- The dismantling of the Soviet Union, with (initially, at least) a minimum of bloodshed.

- The dismantling of the Berlin Wall. (I have a piece of it on my worktable, spontaneously offered by a generous colleague who must intuitively have grasped my deep appreciation of symbols.)

- The election of an activist playwright, Vaclav Havel, as the president of the formerly communist state of Czechoslovakia.

- The election of a union organizer, Lech Walesa, as president of the formerly communist state of Poland.

- The establishment of a formal peace process between Israel and the Palestinian people.

It is fashionable to downplay or dismiss some of these developments because they appear to have proven less dramatic or transformative than was first hoped. The 1992 global warming agreement has been lived up to by almost no one; Al Gore has been a far less visible champion of the environment than most of us expected; the citizens of Kettleman City are still dealing with the issue of a hazardous waste landfill; Lech Walesa proved human, fallible, and political; Vaclav Havel could not prevent the division of his country into two separate states; the Palestinian-Israeli relationship has been staggered by the Rabin assassination, by the subsequent Israeli election and the renewed construction of settlements on the West Bank, and by the actions of Palestinian extremists; plans for the Ward Valley nuclear waste dump in California still periodically inch forward; the deep racial and ethnic divisions in South Africa — among blacks as much as between blacks and whites — continue to threaten the country's stability; Russia has shown some signs of reverting to an aggressive nationalism and has been massively incapable of dealing with its economic and environmental problems, many of which are at near-catastrophic levels.

These apparent failures subtract exactly nothing from the initial successes.

In the universe of the creator, where the energies of the creative process are developed through the simultaneous envisioning of new realities and the accurate accounting of realities already in existence, *prior success and prior failure are two distinct categories.* The objective acknowledgment of successes already achieved builds momentum toward further success; the objective recognition of failure-to-date is a separate activity that *equally* promotes long-term success because it too contributes to the structural tension between what is aimed at and what is at hand.

Most activists are not familiar with this principle. For the good of the transcendent, creative process in which we are engaged, and for the sake of our own mental health and well-being, we need to work with it much more. If we are to propel ourselves and the world forward — and the holographic model of life argues that these aims are finally identical — we must pay greater and more clinical attention to the progress that has been and is being made. Go back and consider the astounding nature of the above list of profoundly positive developments of the last decade, which is only a fraction — an infinitesimal fraction — of what might be written. We cannot afford to undervalue or carelessly overlook progress. We cannot afford to allow setbacks to intrude on an honest evaluation of our successes, great and small. Nor can we afford to miss the unique opportunity to transform momentary failure by incorporating it in a deliberate process of establishing and promoting structural tension — thereby increasing and intensifying the creative energy available to manifest a worthy vision.

There is a nearly legendary activist, someone whose courage I have greatly admired, with whom I once had a revealing conversation. Probably in response to some well-intended compliment of mine, he said, a bit shortly, "There are no heroes." My sense at the time, though I was slightly startled by the comment, was to let the dialogue end there for the moment. Afterward I pondered his statement.

This individual once risked his life on a daily basis and over an extended period of time to document an environmental injustice that subsequently gained international publicity — largely through his efforts — one that has since been significantly addressed by the world community. He is someone of whom my friend and former colleague Peter Dykstra of CNN has said (while admitting that interaction with this person can be enormously trying), "Give me fifty major environmental issues, and fifty of him, and I'll know that at least forty-five of those issues will be taken care of within five years." This activist has thus some intimate acquaintance with what most of us would consider heroism, and any comments by him on the subject should be treated with respect.

Nevertheless, I could not agree with him. I thought for a while about how to respond, and a little after our initial exchange, when I happened to cross his bow again, I said, "You're wrong about heroes, you know. There are a lot of them. What about anyone who understands that she or he has a mission in life, and decides to fulfill it?"

He looked at me as if I had just emerged from a spaceship and said curtly, "But of course. Of course they do that." From his tone it was abundantly clear that he did not mean "Of course such people are heroes." He meant "Those people aren't heroes. *Of course* they accept their missions; we're all obliged to do that. Anyone who doesn't is barely worthy of our attention."

It was an interesting glimpse of the view from one extreme edge of the activist cosmos.

The majority of human beings throughout history have not in fact accepted a personal mission in life, or felt that doing so was an inherent obligation. Had they taken up that gauntlet, the world would be in a much different and improved condition. The material base from which we build today is instead the product of human activities that have largely been based in diversion or distraction from mission, rather than its pursuit. The activist with whom I spoke may in that sense have been correct in regarding acceptance of mission as a kind of moral obligation,

all the more so today, given the intense need for radically transformed relationships (among human beings and between humans and the earth) that can likely be achieved only through the
missionary commitment of many. I suspect, though, that however overly romantic may be our traditional view of heroism, we
are not going to enhance the ranks of those dedicated to transforming the world by denying that heroism exists.

Perhaps we should indeed revise our criteria for the title of
hero. But I do not think we should eliminate the category. The
phenomenon of heroism does exist, and I have seen it close at
hand, from the kitchen tables of working families to the protest-
bannered facades of government buildings, from the stinking
outfalls of chemical plants and stacks of rusted incinerators to
the shadowed gates of nuclear weapons factories, to the bright
display of a traveling solar photovoltaic generator. I have seen it
wherever people — especially ordinary people with an extraordinary love of possibility — have chosen to stand in the way of
the blind and groping forces of ignorant habit, and to stand *for*
an illuminated, transformative commitment to real creativity.
Yes, there are heroes, and most of them are unsung. And it ought
to be a primary focus of the activist ethic to help the hero of the
particular situation to become the hero of the full epic: to offer
the means by which that person, having risen to the isolated occasion, may happily expand her or his horizons so as to become
the person who fully realizes her or his own spirit here, to the infinite benefit of all of us and of the Garden Planet.

The stunning opportunity to *save time*, in the deep sense outlined in the famous *Course in Miracles*, surely hinges on the willingness of individuals to rise beyond themselves — not just on
isolated occasions, but in a greater sense.[3] An activism that pro-

ceeds from Robert Fritz's orientation of the creative, not from the less powerful stances of knee-jerk reactivity or even clever responsiveness, will represent such a genuine self-realization on the part of thousands or millions of people. The opportunity and even the likelihood of such a movement has been building everywhere, from churches and synagogues to personal growth workshops to the private discussions of those activists who have believed that there must be a more effective and powerful means or method or orientation by which to accomplish their worthy ends.

The so-called race to save the planet, along with the race to establish peace and justice and equity among peoples, is not quite a race, and not wholly dependent on the speed of our *reaction* to actual or impending catastrophe. The unspoken question in the hearts of activists everywhere — Is there still time? — has its place and function. Yet it betrays a limited perspective in the sense that time is, or can be, a more flexible commodity than most of us have been trained to believe. It bends and shifts in ways that may evoke awe and wonder in even the most detached and sophisticated astrophysicist. It favors the truly creative, extending to them that latitude which Thoreau extolled as the "license of a higher order of beings." And it favors those who are brave, not in the sense of melodrama but in the genuinely dramatic sense of recognizing the beauty of their opportunities and the uniquely individual vision to which they were born, and of *acting* on that recognition.

Certainly there is still time. If those of us who say we are committed to the vision of Eden show ourselves willing to learn and put into practice those principles by which the Garden would have originally been shaped, time may perfectly well be with us in a transcendent sense. But it will mean accepting that period of disorientation which accompanies the relinquishment of familiar formulas for living — formulas many of us do not even like to admit we have. It will mean opening ourselves to the terrifying possibility that we really are, after all, just beginners, no matter how much we know or believe we have accomplished to date. As Marianne Williamson points out, we cling to familiar ways of thinking and doing because we are afraid accepting new ways would render us *more* powerful, not because we are afraid that letting go of the old ways would make us *less* so.

Considered from that Polynesian perspective illuminated by Margaret Mead, of a mysterious past which remains open and indistinct, the Garden may or may not ever have existed before. But that same tradition tells us that it is utterly real in the future, where it waits, resting on some faith that we will individually or together prepare a place for it *here, now*. It is borne on our thoughts and visions. It will be *born* through the midwifery of our willingness to learn and our humblest acts of commitment.

Notes

Chapter Two

[1] A strong suggestion of the true function of drama, and an endorsement of Arthur Miller's comment, was implied in Christopher Reeve's memorable address at the 1996 Academy Awards. Ironically, Steven Spielberg has come closer to this mark than all but a handful of popularly successful directors, especially with *Schindler's List;* and yet many conscientiously "green" Hollywood celebrities avoided the Playa Vista issue like the plague because, rightly or wrongly, they feared reprisal from a man who had won an Oscar for making a film about the pull of conscience.

[2] The greatest compliment I may have received as an actor came from a friend who got lost while driving around on errands after seeing my "stage portrait" of Thoreau: the philosophical and spiritual matters raised in the show so preoccupied him that he couldn't keep his mind on where he'd planned to go.

[3] Alfred Hitchcock was infamous for making this analogy specific. Such treatment is likely to continue until actors take some sort of united stand on behalf of their own collective spiritual dignity. Thus far, it's all the various actors' unions can do to gather the membership behind issues pertaining to their material welfare.

[4] Including interaction with disease-producing organisms routinely perceived as "hostile" in intent, though they are fundamentally incapable of intention much beyond their own survival.

[5] Conversely, few things haunt the organization more than lapses in its assessment of specific situations. See the discussion, in

Chapter 8, of the Brent Spar oil platform pollution analysis — where a valid campaign was to a degree jeopardized by inaccurate (and finally unnecessary) data.

Chapter Three

[1] In two noteworthy examples of synchronicity, not long after writing this passage I came upon 1) a David Frost television interview with the late Jacques Cousteau, who used the symphony metaphor not merely for life on the earth, but for life throughout the universe — "The symphony," he said, "is huge" — and 2) a Monitor Radio interview with Skylab astronaut Jack Lousma, who said of his 1973 spacewalk, "You can see the painted deserts — painted just the way the Master Painter painted them so many years ago."

Chapter Four

[1] Witness the challenge, for example, of mobilizing the public to respond to attempts in the 104th Congress to undermine the Clean Water Act, the Safe Drinking Water Act, the Endangered Species Act, and other vital environmental legislation — even though polls showed that eighty percent of Americans were concerned about the environment. These assaults on good and popular laws were fed in part by the backlash against an environmentalism perceived by many as melodramatic. Thus swings the pendulum in the realm of the reactive-responsive, and it leaves a goodly number of otherwise enlightened activists sympathizing far too well — and empathizing far too much — with Sisyphus.

[2] It is true that the public may, in its conscious or unconscious wisdom, forgive the manipulative excesses of activists when vital issues are truly at stake. This reasoned or innate generosity does not excuse us from minimizing, and in the end eliminating, the abuse. When we have used the imagery of disaster to excess, we have triggered a short-term psychological and emotional mechanism at the risk of the deeper and longer-term needs of the human spirit. The native resilience of spirit is no excuse at all for diverting it from its natural course.

[3] The phrase "deep creativity" should not be confused with or even assumed to have an intrinsic connection to the phrase "deep ecology." I make this point because as an environmental activist I might be expected by many readers to be a student or proponent of the latter. That is only partly true, as will probably become clear in the course of this book.

Chapter Six

[1] In fact, even within Greenpeace itself, today only a handful of people are mindful of the story — a fact which carries some symbolism.

[2] Paul Spong's story is movingly told in Rex Weyler's *Song of the Whale* (1986).

[3] The ultimate linear approach to the reshaping of circumstances and events is to use physical force, and the ultimate example of this approach is war. By this means the greatest quantity of physical force available to human beings is brought to bear in its most concentrated form, which today means nuclear weapons. But the world has actually evolved to a point — witness the Comprehensive Nuclear Test Ban Treaty — where nations at least dimly recognize that such a concentrated application of linear consciousness is inherently counterproductive. You cannot build a better world by destroying or threatening to destroy this one; you cannot *impose* a "new world order" worthy of the name.

[4] The possibility of twenty-six dimensions is mentioned in Stephen Hawking's *A Brief History of Time* (1988), in a discussion of string theories (p. 164). I encountered the other figures years ago, in a book whose title and author I regret to say I have since forgotten.

[5] If the creationists would relax their death grip on the wondrous imagery of the Old Testament for a minute, they might notice that science has been forced round to a variety of conclusions that endorse the bedrock perceptions (though not the literal interpretation) of all the great religions. The "Big Bang" theory, for example, is about as ringing an endorsement of the core concept of Genesis

(a good chunk of it, anyway) as anyone has a right to expect of a motley group of humans operating primarily from the left half of their brains.

Chapter Seven

[1] It is only practical to state that an activist institution like Greenpeace can clearly have its most powerful, long-term impact through its influence on the deep patterns in a culture rather than through manipulating the outward results or products of such patterns. For example, though industry has often challenged Greenpeace to have alternative technologies in hand before protesting destructive corporate practices, and the organization has done a remarkable job in this regard, it is absurd to suggest that it be held responsible for doing R & D (research and development) for the whole corporate universe. Though it is among the largest and best-known nonprofit enterprises in the world, its size and budget are minuscule compared to those of the companies and governmental bureaucracies it regularly confronts. See the comment from CNN's Peter Dykstra, in Chapter 11, on Greenpeace's annual expenditures.

Chapter Nine

[1] The practical awareness of an intuitive faculty among the Indians was noted by Thoreau in *The Maine Woods*; he was strongly impressed by their seemingly inexplicable means of navigating the forest.

[2] There was some drama in the aftermath, however. He had some forgivable hesitation about turning over the tape to the local authorities, who became sufficiently impatient that they broke his door down to get it.

[3] For an incisive account of this incident, and of the entire occupation, see Paul Chaat Smith and Robert Allen Warrior's *Like a Hurricane* (The New Press, 1996). The description of the planned GSA raid and its cancellation is on pp. 67–69.

[4] Nor in the long run did the violence serve the reservation "goon squads" — quietly endorsed by certain of the federals — which,

few people realize, killed many of the "radicals" afterwards and generated something like a civil war on the reservation.

[5] I found the quote (further synchronicity) in a fundraising letter from the American Indian College Fund; my wife placed that day's mail beside me as I was composing the chapter.

[6] Which even Greenpeace has (embarrassingly) quoted without correcting the attribution, in a 1995 mailing to contributors. Such misattribution, by the way, is not the screenwriter's fault. The film's producers neglected to clarify the distinction between history and fabrication in the movie's credits. (For a fragment of the original and a breathtaking collection of other Indian oratorical passages, seek out T. C. McLuhan's 1970 *Touch the Earth*.)

[7] I have this article only in an old photocopy, without date or publisher or writer's name, and regret that I cannot be more specific in the attribution.

[8] There are variations within and across many cultures, as Joseph Campbell indicates in *The Power of Myth*.

[9] And this includes a great many nominal activists who favor the psychological comfort of clinging to familiar practices and *ways of thinking*.

Chapter Ten

[1] This education came partly by way of an effective article by Galen Rowell, "The Agony of Tibet," in the *Greenpeace* magazine of March/April 1990.

Chapter Eleven

[1] Even more clearly related to the theme of a visionary interaction with the media, given the close connection between the media and the world of publishing, is the process by which I came to write this book. The opportunity to create the work hinged improbably on a one-line mention of my college lecture tour in a February 1994 edition of the *New York Times Magazine*.

[2] I appreciate the challenge of dealing with swings of the pendu-

lum of popular (and economic) support, having perhaps unwisely allowed the timing of my own departure from Greenpeace to be dictated largely by the mechanics of that pendulum. This does not alter my perception that great organizations, like great individuals, master the ability to transcend those mechanics.

[3] The Cornel West quote is from an interview on *Charlie Rose.* In a workshop I created for activists, I suggest an experimental meeting format for their organizations in which no discussion whatsoever of problems is allowed until after a full-blown exploration of *goals*, beginning with the largest vision to which the group believes it is dedicated, and in which no discussion whatsoever of *means* is allowed until both the exploration of vision and a detailed accounting of existing reality (in both its promising and challenging aspects) are complete.

Chapter Twelve

[1] Although walking through the most beautiful garden on the planet may or may not stimulate an enhanced ethic in the person who does it, the physical act of *planting* a garden has astonishing potential for tapping and maturing the creative processes of the individual. I have seen reports on programs, notably in some inner cities and in certain prisons, that document this. Readers interested in this idea might like to know of the organization Gardens for Humanity, based in Sedona, Arizona, which specializes in promoting the creation of "sustainable healing gardens" in numerous locations, especially "areas left forlorn by the neglect of humankind." It was founded, not coincidentally, by a coalition of artists, gardeners, and healers — including close family of the artist quoted at the beginning of Chapter 1.

[2] In this connection I have often opined from the lectern that there is, after all, a reason why Greenpeace named itself "Greenpeace" and not "The Amalgamated Global Environmental Problem-Solving Society."

[3] It may not be coincidental that the demand for my services as a

speaker fell off after I became more preoccupied with travel and lecturing, and less regularly involved in major direct-action campaign work for Greenpeace.

Chapter Thirteen

[1] For some reason, this passage has been routinely cited as originating in the inaugural address of Nelson Mandela, but it is in fact from Ms. Williamson's 1992 book *A Return to Love.* President Mandela's address (of May 10, 1994) was moving and had much power, but nowhere contained these words or their approximation.

[2] I have used this image for years when speaking about global environmentalism.

[3] The noted reference to time in *A Course in Miracles* (1976) may be found on page 3 of the "Manual for Teachers"; it summarizes the mission of the "teachers of God" in the statement "Their function is to save time." I encountered this quotation under unusual circumstances some years ago. Late in my former career as a performer, I was portraying a singularly terrible minister in a film about the Salem witch trials, shot on historical location. (Interestingly, my involvement in acting had begun with a closely related role in Arthur Miller's *The Crucible,* in high school.) Someone left a copy of the *Course* on a table in the actors' holding area. As I had already begun teaching the principles of creativity by that time, I naturally opened to the section of the book that dealt with teaching. The quotation about saving time struck me almost immediately. It is no surprise to me that shortly thereafter I set aside acting for activism.

Acknowledgments

It's likely that I would never have come to write this book, nor have pursued my present career in activism, but for the teachings of Robert Fritz, who has challenged thousands to take up the reins of their lives in the most powerful way. I once read an article about a woman who assisted laryngectomy patients in regaining the power of speech; the piece was called, approximately, "The Angel Who Could Make Men Swear." Robert's intensity has been known to provoke a similar response, but his work stands with the most important on the planet.

I am honored by and deeply grateful for the foreword to this book by His Holiness the Dalai Lama; I would also like to express my thanks to his secretary, Tenzin Geyche Tethong, and to Lobsang Tenphell, for their assistance in making the foreword possible and in providing material for the chapter on the Tibetan situation and the Dalai Lama's vision.

Any good book requires a good editor — or two. I was blessed with the latter. First, Deanne Urmy offered me the opportunity to create the work and shepherded it through the completion of the original manuscript while dealing with a very full slate of other concerns. Second, Amy Caldwell brought to bear an incisive gift for both condensing the work and reconfiguring key passages to have the greatest impact. She exercised these skills thoughtfully and patiently even while under significant pressure of time, for which I thank her. My thanks also to Chris Kochansky for her excellent and painstaking work as copy editor.

My wise and kindly spouse, Elizabeth Anne Dickinson, and several of our dearest friends offered deep encouragement from the project's inception. Elizabeth's intuition led directly to the book's foreword; I am also grateful for both her general and her particular commentary on various drafts. I am grateful as well to Cathyann Swindlehurst for her early endorsement and suggestions, and to Rondalyn Whitney for her timely enthusiasm. My erstwhile colleague and onetime cellmate Mark Floegel, and as well friends Todd Conatser, Charles Skinner, Chris Oatis-Skinner, Allaire Paterson-Koslo, and Oliver Muirhead, each reviewed some or all of the original manuscript. I appreciate their time and input.

Certain incidents, images, and concepts I have related or employed originated with colleagues and friends who were gracious enough to share them. My particular thanks to Red Elk and Sweet Image, to Doree Seronde, and to others who prefer anonymity, for allowing the use of personal anecdotes in these pages. Thanks also to Henry and Mimi Smith for the time they took to discuss their activist experiences and to comment on my interpretation of historical events. I would also like to acknowledge my brother, musician, activist, and writer Peter Childs, for first bringing to my attention the analogy of the hologram as employed by Al Gore.

Other people and institutions offering material assistance and support in the completion of this book include: the Seattle Public Library; Dr. Kalen Hamann; LaDawna Howard and Joe Distante; Claire Bloom; Robert Dhondrup; Peter Dykstra; Leigh Bloom; David Bigley; the South African Consulate General; Nancy Brown of Friends of the Everglades; Don Littlefield; the Army Corps of Engineers, Public Affairs Department; Anna Copeland; Southeast Asian Information Network; the Los Angeles Public Library; NASA; Kelly Quirke; Bill Walker; Faith Childs; David Rich of Strategic Events International and his colleagues on the staff of Lordly & Dame, Inc.; Carol Anthony; Nora McCarthy; Rex Weyler; Bradley Angel; Tom Lent; Ted and Bill Flanigan of IRT Publications/The Results Center; Richard Heede of the Rocky Mountain Institute; Jacques Seronde of Gardens for Humanity; and all those who responded to an informal survey on titles. I am also grateful to the friends and students with whom I have discussed concepts contained herein, and whose responses have helped me refine many of my ideas.

Finally, I wish to express my deep thanks to the scores of activists — whether from Greenpeace or other large organizations, or from the smallest community groups — alongside whom I have been privileged to work during the past fifteen years, on whose efforts rest the many experiences cited in, or influential in the evolution of, this work.